"In her signature style, Ann gives the ingredients necessary for graceful leadership. Always listening, learning, and serving, a leader knows that great things happen in service to others. There's no chance that you forget this leadership truth after reading Ann's thoughts!"

—Vincent J. Costanza, superintendent in residence
Teaching Strategies, LLC

"Ann McClain Terrell's *Graceful Leadership in Early Childhood Education* is a spiritual, autobiographical homage to all the women on whose shoulders she stands—those who have inspired her to develop grit, vision, and tenacity and the wisdom to lead with grace, courage, and commitment. This book is a must read for those who want to be inspired to lead and inspire others."

—Maurice Sykes, executive director
Early Childhood Leadership Institute
and author of *Doing the Right Thing for Children:
Eight Qualities of Leadership*

GRACEFUL LEADERSHIP
IN EARLY CHILDHOOD EDUCATION

Graceful Leadership

in Early Childhood Education

Ann McClain Terrell

Redleaf Press®
www.redleafpress.org
800-423-8309

Published by Redleaf Press
10 Yorkton Court
St. Paul, MN 55117
www.redleafpress.org

First edition 2018
Cover design by Jim Handrigan
Cover photograph by Latoya Gayle Studios
Interior design by Douglas Schmitz and Jim Handrigan
Typeset in Palatino
Printed in the United States of America
25 24 23 22 21 20 19 18   1 2 3 4 5 6 7 8

Library of Congress Cataloging-in-Publication Data
Names: Terrell, Ann McClain, author.
Title: Graceful leadership in early childhood education / Ann McClain Terrell.
Description: First edition. | St. Paul, MN : Redleaf Press, 2018. | Includes
    bibliographical references.
Identifiers: LCCN 2018006972 (print) | LCCN 2018028180 (ebook) | ISBN
    9781605545745 (ebook) | ISBN 9781605545738 (pbk. : alk. paper)
Subjects: LCSH: Early childhood education. | Educational leadership.
Classification: LCC LB1139.25 (ebook) | LCC LB1139.25 .M46 2018 (print) | DDC
    372.21--dc23
LC record available at https://lccn.loc.gov/2018006972

Printed on acid-free paper

This book is dedicated to the women who raised me

and raised me up and on whose shoulders I stand:

my mother, Patricia Jane Small Terrell;

my grandmothers, Mayme Lee McClain Small

and Wilma Dickerson Terrell;

and my great-grandmother,

Annie Bell Kimbrough Terrell,

affectionately known as Momma,

Mama Mayme, Big Mama, and Little Mama.

I also dedicate this book to my children,

Jenise and Kenisha, of whom I'm so very proud.

They've always allowed me to work on behalf of others.

Their love, patience, and support sustained me

while I took on this project, and it is very

much appreciated.

This book is also dedicated to my grandchildren,

BriAnna, Kenyon, Brian, Brice, and Journee,

who bring much pride and joy to my life.

I love you all!

Contents

Acknowledgments

Thank you to my elders for their wisdom and my ancestors who have guided me throughout my life and career.

Thank you to my "community" of relatives, colleagues, mentors, and mentees who provided the experiences and education that I draw upon in the pages of this book.

Thank you to Holly Elissa Bruno, who has never wavered in her belief that writing this book was an important step for me and that I should consider risking becoming more visible.

Thank you to my cousins, those wonderful Dickerson women, especially Martha (Dot) and Estelle, who modeled for me true grace and dignity.

Thank you to my daddy's brothers, my Uncle Alonzo and Uncle Richard, who were the real father figures in my life, especially my Uncle Richard, who taught me the true meaning of family and family history and so many other life lessons during our road trips together home to Kentucky.

Thank you to my Aunt Betsy, the current matriarch of my mother's side of the family. I have enjoyed spending more time with you and getting to know you and Cousin Muriel better.

Thank you to the teams I've been fortunate enough to lead and to the new leaders I've had the pleasure of working with, especially Tamara Johnson, Kortney Smith, Tanya Johnson, Delechia Johnson, Sonja Smith, and Candace Armstrong; I'm grateful for the lessons you all have taught me.

Thank you to Laura Saterfield and Jill Haglund for your steadfast friendship and collegiality throughout the years.

Thank you to Dr. Florence Johnson for your ever-present support of me and my work.

Thank you to Mell and Angie Monroe, owners of the Welcome Inn Manor, who provided me with the environment to write and the freedom of their Chicago B&B.

Thank you to the five "Sisters with Amazing Grace" (SWAG) who invited me to lunch and fellowship with them that spring day at the National Museum of African American History and Culture while they were there as part of their sixtieth birthday celebrations.

Thank you to my current and former Redleaf Press family. Thank you Kyra Ostendorf for reaching out to me with an idea. Thank you Kara Lomen for encouraging and cajoling. Thank you Mari Kesselring for embracing my work with such understanding and commitment. Thank you to Jim Handrigan, Douglas Schmitz, Sue Ostfield, and Nicole Borneman. Finally, David Heath, thank you for your ever-present support, patience, and belief in me.

I thank you all for your part in my journey.

Preface

I never thought I would write a book. But sometimes life gives you opportunities that are worth seizing, even if they are outside your comfort zone. In 2013 I was a candidate on the slate of early childhood professionals campaigning for election to the Governing Board of the National Association for the Education of Young Children (NAEYC). After the "Meet the Candidates" session at the national conference, I was approached by Kyra Ostendorf, then an acquisitions editor for Redleaf Press. She asked me if I'd ever considered writing a book. I think Kyra may have been intrigued by a fact I shared during the session that I was one of the first people in Milwaukee, Wisconsin, to be approved to care for children under the age of two in an out-of-home setting. But her question threw me completely off guard. Writing a book was one thing that has never been on my to-do list. I guess Kyra saw the dazed look on my face because she went on to say that my passion and voice were so clear, she believed that others could gain insight from my experiences and life lessons.

I was flattered by the idea, but writing a book meant sharing myself and my life and career experiences with others. It took me a while to come to the decision to take this step. In fact, I literally ignored Kyra for over a year. Then one day, one of the women I mentor said to me that I should do it so that others could learn from the same valuable lessons she'd learned from me. So began this part of my leadership journey.

What has been *your* leadership journey? What's lighted your path along the way? What challenges have you had to hurdle? Were there any unexpected opportunities, twists, turns, or forks in the road? Did you follow the signposts or blaze a new trail? Regardless of our position in leadership, we all have stories about our journeys; some are success stories and some are tales of challenges, but all include lessons.

In this book, I will share some of my professional journey and the lessons I've learned along the way. But my leadership journey is not a path I've walked alone, so this book will also introduce some of my family, friends, and colleagues that have had an impact on my career. I hope the lessons from my leadership journey help guide you and that this book becomes one of those "keepers," a resource you turn to when there is a challenge in your leadership journey that needs tackling or when you just want to reflect on your leadership journey.

Within these pages are my lessons learned, parables, so to speak, about discovering my voice while maintaining my way of being in this world. You will read about how I discovered my voice, honed it, spoke my truth, and finally sang my song along this leadership journey. Writing this book has been a cathartic process for me and an act of love, my way of lighting others' candles.

During my career, I've known some people that hold their information or knowledge close to them and have been not willing to share at all. I'm the opposite of that. People that know or work with me will tell you that if I have information that will benefit them personally or professionally, I will happily share it with them. I'm a firm believer that sharing our knowledge with others makes all of us and our work and community stronger. If I light your candle with mine, it doesn't diminish my flame. Instead, it creates a brighter way for us all. It reminds me of the verse from the children's song that became popular during the 1960s civil rights era: "This little light of mine, I'm going to let it shine."

People have always been a great source of inspiration for me. I find inspiration other places too. What has inspired and encouraged you on your leadership journey? I love the Amazing Grace series of books by Mary

Hoffman with illustrations by various artists, including Caroline Binch, June Allan, Cornelius Van Wright, and Ying-Hwa Hu. I was quite happy to watch Grace "grow up" in the subsequent books, *Boundless Grace*, *Starring Grace*, *Encore Grace*, *Bravo Grace*, *Princess Grace*, and the newest *Grace at Christmas*. (Apparently, I've made no secret about my enthusiasm for this series. In 2013 members of my staff gave me a birthday present of the whole series of books, a copy of the version adapted for the stage, and the Amazing Grace paper dolls!) As a child of the '60s and young adult of the '70s, I think it was the message of the original book that resonated with me. You see, Grace, very much like a young Ann, loved reading; however, Grace also enjoyed acting out the stories she read in her backyard with friends or on stage at school with her classmates. The story goes that there came a time when Grace wanted to play Peter Pan in her school play but was told by some of her classmates that she could not act in that role because she was a girl *and* because she was African American. Needless to say, her classmates' viewpoint left Grace confused, hurt, and immensely disappointed. Well, Grace's wise grandmother steps in and shows her that she can be anything she wants to be and chooses to work hard to be. In each of the subsequent books, Grace tackles a life challenge, and the lessons she learns are good not only for the young reader but for us all. My friend and colleague Chris Amirault (2017) says the book *Amazing Grace* is "a deeply human book discussing a number of issues related to family, culture and identity in honest, thoughtful ways."

My hope is that my book does the same for early childhood education leaders, and any leader or emerging leader, as the *Amazing Grace* books have done for young people. That is, it provides a look into the complexities, challenges, and opportunities of leadership through that same lens of family, culture, and identity.

CHAPTER 1

Be Still and Listen

The term *grace* is not often, if ever, associated with leadership. Leadership is often equated with dominance and ferocity, position and power. In this viewpoint, there are winners and losers. But it is time we understand that leadership can also be gentle and firm. It can be graceful, allowing for both the dignity of the leader and those being led. With graceful leadership, we all learn and grow together. We raise the boats of all. We light one another's candles. In the *Harvard Business Review* article "What Women Know about Leadership that Men Don't," Tony Schwartz writes, "[Women] bring to leadership a more complete range of the qualities modern leaders need, including self-awareness, emotional attunement, humility and authenticity" (2012). This is graceful leadership.

While Schwartz's statement is only about women, men can also possess or learn to incorporate some of these attributes into their leadership style, especially the capacity for emotional intelligence. Dr. J. D. Andrews was a man who worked in the field of early childhood education for thirty years with leadership roles at the National Association for the Education of Young

Children (NAEYC), the Council for Professional Recognition, and Head Start. While I did not have the privilege of meeting J. D., many of the people I hold in high regard did know and work with him. J. D. passed away in December 2016, and those who knew, worked with, and loved him participated in a celebration of life memorial service at NAEYC headquarters in March 2017. The program from the service included "often heard lessons from J. D." One lesson in particular stands out in relationship to graceful leadership: "True leaders go beyond beliefs and thoughts and inspire others to translate visions into reality." The words his colleagues used to describe him included *visionary*, *mentor*, *trailblazer*, *activist*, *thinker*, and *friend*. The words that J. D.'s colleagues used to describe him are also some of the characteristics of a graceful leader.

What Is Grace?

One dictionary definition of *grace* is "simple elegance or refinement of movement" as in elegance, poise, or finesse or a "polite manner of behaving." It also defines *grace* in Christian terms as "the free and unmerited favor of God as manifested in the bestowal of blessings." One can display graceful leadership by carrying themselves with quiet confidence, being respectful of others, and supporting others in their professional growth and development. Grace is not just religious favor or a prayer said before a meal; it is a way of life and leading.

Good leaders are reflective people. The ability to self-reflect, to give serious thought about your own beliefs and behaviors, is an admirable quality and one that all leaders, and those intending to be graceful leaders, should possess. Early childhood teacher trainer and educator Deb Curtis (2017) says, "To study yourself is among the most important professional development tasks you can take up." Indeed, a defining attribute of leadership is to fundamentally understand who we are and what drives and motivates us as individuals to act. Once we better understand ourselves, we can be contemplative before acting or responding, as great leaders do.

"A quiet woman is often mistaken as one

who is weak, feeble, and easily influenced.

In reality, she is one who understands

her feelings, thoughts, and ideas can be

conveyed just as effectively with softly

spoken words. . . . She does not actively

seek attention. Rather, she allows her

presence alone to draw others, as a true

lady is aware and quite confident that

those who surround her will take notice."

—Sassy Tammy

The Grace in Self-Reflection

When I reflect on my own experience with graceful leadership, the grace that has often been attributed to me is, I believe, a characteristic that I inherited from my grandmother Mayme Lee Small. When she passed away, during her funeral repast, several of the Amish people who reside in our small Kentucky hometown brought food to our family home as a gesture of compassion during our mourning. When I answered the door, the woman who led the group handed me the food and said that my grandmother was one of the most dignified people that she'd ever met.

My grandmother was indeed a quiet woman, dedicated to her family and community. She modeled for me the quality of self-reflection. She was a contemplative woman, and I still have a visual memory of her in deep thought as she stood staring out of the window above the kitchen sink of her home. I recall her and my other female elders saying to me and other children, "Go somewhere, sit down, and be still." That admonishment typically meant that we were being overly active and getting into situations that we shouldn't have been. However, that direction—to stop and take a moment to reflect, to ponder our actions or behavior—was some of the best advice I've ever received. When I got older and was myself a mother and also had enough professional experience to appreciate this advice, I wrote a poem about it:

> Momma used to say and
> Mama Mayme and Big Momma used to say and
> Little Momma used to say,
> "Go somewhere, *sit down* and be still . . ."
> "Go somewhere, sit down and *be still* . . ."
> Little did I know then what I know now about
> The power and peace that comes when I
> Go somewhere, sit down and be still.

In her 1993 book *Sisters of the Yam,* author bell hooks advises that "Black women have not focused sufficiently on our need for contemplative spaces. We are often 'too busy' to find time for solitude. And yet it is in the stillness that we also learn how to be with ourselves in a spirit of acceptance and peace. Then when we re-enter community, we are able to extend this acceptance to others. Without knowing how to be alone, we cannot know how to be with others and sustain the necessary autonomy" (186).

Now that is amazing grace—being able to extend acceptance and peace to others!

My friend and colleague Valora Washington once wrote to me, "I always admire you so much! You exude a quiet strength and determination that gets stuff done!" I believe the quiet strength that she sees exhibited is there because I do take that time that bell hooks calls the "contemplative space" and stillness. My alone time is as essential to my spirit and as necessary to my soul as food and sleep are to my body. Even early in my career, when my children were young and in early elementary school, they were often anxious to talk about their day when we got home in the evening after school and work. I'd ask them to go to their bedrooms for a short period of time. I explained to them that I would be all theirs after that. I'd usually quietly sit with a cup of coffee in front of the television while the news was on and take the time to process the day and think about and plan for the next day. After about thirty minutes, I'd call my children to the kitchen where I was preparing our evening meal, and we'd talk about their day and their homework.

> *Sign hung on my office door: "Sometimes*
>
> *I get so tired . . . then I think about what*
>
> *Harriet Tubman did for a living."*

Taking this time for ourselves to be still is more important than most leaders realize. Many women leaders, especially women of color, have had negative experiences in the workplace that leave us feeling like we need to be careful and protect ourselves in those environments. It's challenging to be the only woman or person of color in the room. In these environments, our decisions or input may be questioned; we may be undermined, overlooked, and underestimated. That feeling also comes when others take credit for your work, act like you're not in the room, or are dismissive of your input. Have you ever been in a situation where you present an idea and no one paid attention to it, but a while later someone else says the same thing and everyone thinks it's a good idea?

Black women have often been characterized as angry. It seems that whenever we express ourselves in ways that don't allow us to be doormats or seen as exotic, oversexed women, we're labeled *angry*. We're not angry. We're often just tired, tired of giving from an empty cup. Take that quiet time, at least fifteen to thirty minutes each day, to get still and ask yourself, "How did the day go?" "What can I do differently tomorrow?" or, depending on the situation, "Who am I?" and "Do I like the work I'm doing?" "Is this the work I'm supposed to be doing?" "Is the work I'm doing truly my career or a calling?"

The majority of my career has been in the field of early childhood education; however, I've come to believe that my calling is to be a "builder" or an influencer, working quietly to make an impact.

These questions and that reflective time allows you to begin to refill your cup. Taking this time is vital for your well-being. As a leader, you must take care of yourself in order to serve or lead others. Enthusiasm and energy is contagious, and the members of your team will pick up your energy and enthusiasm. I've observed early childhood programs where a change in leadership resulted in a change in the staff's work performance. The former leader was energetic, charismatic, and held high expectations for the program and the children and families served. The new leader brought a different nonchalant energy to the program, and the quality of care became somewhat laissez-faire.

Confusion and chaos in your personal or professional life presses you to reflect and make decisions in order to move your life forward. For those of us in leadership positions, we need harmony of spirit and to be in touch with our own feelings so that we can motivate others. Have you experienced one of those moments of destiny when your body and spirit are aligned and you know this is what you're supposed to be doing? But as my friend Maurice Sykes (2014, 83) says, "A broken spirit cannot lift another broken spirit." In times of confusion or stress, I find that I need to get organized—that is, to have some method of putting things in order. I will often find some way of channeling this decision-making process. My children would sometimes jokingly say things like, "Something's going on; Mom's cleaning out the closet." I typically find an activity that represents "cleaning up" or "clearing out." I use that energy and time to think and work through whatever challenge I'm facing. I make mental and written notes about next steps in my problem-solving process.

Often leadership happens in those quiet or private moments, the thoughts in bed that keep you up or wake you up at night. It takes more time and energy to be confused and confounded, stressed and overwhelmed, than to "get still and listen." If you take the time to do this, the information will come to you, and you will make a decision. Then you must write it down and put your energy behind the decision you've made. Make a plan and goals—you have the stuff you need to win the struggle. Change begins at the end of your comfort zone.

> *"[My mother] would greet us pleasantly*
>
> *and immediately she seemed to surround*
>
> *the chaotic atmosphere of morning strife*
>
> *with something of order, of efficient and*
>
> *quiet uniformity, so that one had the*
>
> *feeling that life was small and curiously*
>
> *ordered."*
>
> *—Meridel Le Sueur,*
>
> Ripening: Selected Work

Years of practicing "get still and listen" have served me well in my career. A colleague of mine sent me a wonderful note after a particularly successful event she'd led. "Good morning, Ann," she wrote. "I want to personally thank you so much for not only your immense help through this process but the style in which you offered your support. Your calm, strong spirit offers me a sense of security and extended grace; it is unmatched! I love being in your presence!"

The time you take to get still and listen will be worth it in the end. It will make decision making less stressful for you, and others may notice how much thought you put behind each decision you make.

Adapting to Change

One of my friends gave me the nickname "Quiet Storm." One day Jenise, my older daughter, called me and said, "I give up. Are we that much alike?" Smugly smiling to myself because I knew the answer was yes, I answered her question with the question, "Why?" She shared that some of her work colleagues had dubbed her with the nickname "Quiet Storm." On the phone, sounding somewhat inquisitive and puzzled at the same time, she said, "And they don't even know you." She indeed has inherited my quiet, contemplative persona. My younger daughter, Kenisha, on the other hand, is my outgoing, "doesn't meet a stranger" daughter who wears her emotions on her sleeves. We used to joke in our house, "telephone, telegraph, tell Kenisha!" My daughters' high school counselor asked me one day how I managed to raise two daughters who are so different yet still very confident and comfortable with who they are as individuals. I explained to her that I love them equally and raised them the same, but I hopefully gave each of them what they needed as individuals and respected them as individuals. As their mother, I am most proud of the fact that they are not only sisters but are also friends.

Another colleague has used the term *still water* to describe me. I think that *still water* and *quiet storm* are both appropriate characterizations of me and my way of being in this world, especially given that I'm a Pisces by birth and "still waters run deep," as the saying goes.

Water is fluid and, in its stillness, reflective. When I was growing up, Black people who found success working within the larger community prided themselves in being able to *code switch*. This term referred to the ability to not only speak the language of the Black community, but also the ability to move inside the greater, and usually whiter, community. One day, several years ago, I heard a young woman correct someone who had used this term. She said something like, "We now refer to that as being *fluid*; it's a more acceptable and positive term than *code switching*."

Martha Beck (accessed 2018), noted life coach and author, advises people in challenging situations to "Relax. Stay fluid. Get still. Reflect. Be water, my friend." This advice can be especially empowering when it comes to change in one's life. We all experience change and manage change in different ways. You will certainly face changes in your professional life as you navigate your leadership journey. All change is emotional and includes some loss *and* growth. But challenges allow us to discover things about ourselves. I have a friend that once said to me that I have the amazing ability to continuously reinvent myself. I don't think I've reinvented myself; I think I've been fluid enough to adapt to change—including, and maybe especially, change in my professional life. Life isn't static, and without challenge there is no growth. In fact, resisting challenge and change can prevent success.

> *"When the rhythm of the drumbeat*
>
> *changes, the dance steps must adapt."*
>
> *—African proverb*

Change can be positive or it can be negative. If you're dealing with loss, of course change is more challenging and will probably take more time to deal with than perhaps a positive change. The death of a loved one is more challenging to deal with than a promotion at work. However, in both cases, I've found that taking time to be still and reflect helps people to move forward, especially if you are in a leadership role; take the time to listen to that small voice that is always there. Maya Angelou (2014) may have said it best: "Listen to yourself and in that quietude you might hear the voice of God." Find your peace within, meditate on what fills your cup, and focus on what you're grateful for.

Recently there has been a lot of research and discussion about mindfulness for children and adults. As I reflect on mindfulness, it seems to me that it is about being still and getting in tune with and connecting your body and mind. It's about calming yourself down when you feel anxious and focusing your energy. My ancestors knew about the power of mindfulness; they didn't call it that, but they understood it when they'd say, "Go somewhere, sit down, and be still."

Sometimes we need a reminder to be still. Daffodils and peonies are some of my favorite flowers: peonies because they remind me of my maternal grandmother's front yard when I was growing up in Kentucky, and daffodils because their blooming in early spring reminds me that winter is almost over. I used to have a picture of a bright yellow daffodil pinned to the bulletin board that was directly across from my desk. This was my reminder to be still. In times of stress, I would close my office door, focus on that daffodil, and breathe.

Sometimes you may find it necessary to be still, or be quiet, and listen while in a group situation. Some may interpret this as your not contributing to the meeting; however, in reality, you are conducting yourself in the manner that allows you to be most productive. Have you ever experienced a meeting discussion where some of the attendees are intimidated or afraid to share their thoughts? Or a meeting where one or two people take over the conversation? The graceful act of listening to what is being communicated by others and then sharing your thoughts on the subject at hand is an act of leadership and says to others, especially if there are subordinates in the discussion, that what they have to say is as valued as the thoughts of others at the table. I've been blessed with opportunities to serve on or chair many boards, committees, and councils. In these roles, I put forth an effort to make sure that the voices of all who sat around those tables were heard and appreciated. As a member of large group meetings, I found myself being quiet and listening until the time was right for the input that I had. During my term on the Governing Board of NAEYC, I often used this method of communicating with my colleagues. I waited patiently until others had their opportunity to share and then would offer my thoughts on the subject at hand. When my term on the governing board ended, I received a card from the executive director, Rhian Evans Allvin, in which she stated, "When I think of your time on the governing board, I think about your gentle wisdom and calm, steadfast approach to our agenda."

CHAPTER 2

Be Ready for Grace

"Grace is a power that comes in and transforms

a moment to something better."

—*Caroline Myss*, The Wisdom

of Sundays *by Oprah Winfrey*

Anyone who really knows me knows that I'm a fan of college basketball. I make out my March Madness bracket every year, and somehow Kentucky and Louisville always end up in the final four on my bracket! So I'll use a basketball analogy in regard to preparing for and taking advantage of opportunities that will come your way. I used to tell my daughters when they played high school basketball to position themselves to take the shot. Be ready when the ball comes your way; if you've prepared and practiced, and you know the game, then you will have the winning edge. I have been in the "position" to be "graced" with, benefitted from, and had the immense pleasure of participating in some momentous opportunities during my career. Some have been career and life changing.

Embracing Opportunities

In the spring of 1998, I was the coordinator of a campus-based early childhood program at Milwaukee Area Technical College (MATC). We had recently completed the building of what was then considered the state-of-the-art early childhood center, with state licensing, developmentally appropriate practices, and NAEYC accreditation standards all incorporated in the design of the building, the classrooms, and the programming. The lead teachers all had degrees, and the center served both students and community families and children. That year, our campus was selected by then Congressperson Tom Barrett, now mayor of Milwaukee, and his team to host a community forum on child care. The day consisted of panels that were composed of national and local early childhood experts, including Helen Blank, Melinda Green, and Ellen Galinsky. The keynote speaker for the event was then first lady Hillary Rodham Clinton. Well, you can imagine the excitement that all the staff, faculty, and families had when we found out that the event would include a tour of our center by Mrs. Clinton. As the event planning continued, I was notified that the MATC president, Dr. John Birkholz, had selected me to lead the tour for Mrs. Clinton and her entourage. I was joyful and a bit anxious with the promise of this opportunity, and there were others who believed that they were more deserving of this opportunity. This was quite challenging for me because I still needed to work beside or with those who felt the decision to allow me to lead the center tour was disrespectful to them and their positions. Of course, knowing that I had the support of the college president made those days a bit easier, but you can believe that I was challenged in a number of ways in the days leading up to that special event.

The day of the event came, and besides getting over the necessary security detail—including bomb-sniffing dogs and securing one of the bathrooms for the First Lady in case of an emergency (that is when I first heard the term

FLOTUS used)—we were all ready. Mrs. Clinton entered, and as I stood in line with Congressperson Barrett, Senator Herb Kohl, and Dr. Birkholz, we were introduced to the First Lady and the tour began. I was thoroughly impressed with the questions she asked that indicated that she had an in-depth knowledge of the components of high-quality early childhood educational programs. She asked about the child-to-staff ratios and the education levels, salaries, and benefits of the teaching staff. She interacted with the children and families that day, asking about their experiences in the program.

Later that day, during her keynote address, she referenced her experience in the program, thanked me and the staff, and said it was one of the best programs she had seen. The program staff members that were in the auditorium were so very proud to hear her words of praise for the work we were doing. Later I received a handwritten note from the First Lady thanking me for the tour and the gift that our children had presented to her. I will confess here that when Hillary Clinton ran for US president in 2016, I supported her because I understood that she was not one who just read talking points that had been written for her or who just gave lip service to topics about young children, child care, and early childhood education. She understood these issues deeply and would work to improve the state of our field.

This story demonstrates that you never know who is observing your performance at work. By performing my job with integrity, fidelity, and transparency, I made my work noticeable, and I positioned myself to be ready when that opportunity came to me and gracefully accepted it. Are you positioning yourself for an opportunity that may come your way?

Sometimes along your leadership journey, you will encounter people who challenge your right to a position or role. I've found these situations to be some of the most challenging of my career hurdles. At each position I've held, there have been these kinds of challenges, from staff members who challenged my authority and expertise, to board members who protected their nonproductive staff member friends, to individuals who believed the positions I held should've been granted to them. How do you gracefully deal with people who feel entitled to something that you earned? I tried to not allow these challenges to change me and how I "show up" for the work I do.

In some cases, I called on my mentors and cried to them about these situations, and their reassurances sustained me. In other situations, I just turned to my own internal fortitude, what some may call *grit*. I would start and end my day in my car with Yolanda Adams, that wonderful gospel artist, arming myself with the knowledge that the battle was not mine and reminding myself that I just needed to keep my head up, maintain my dignity and work ethic, and perform my best work. As mentioned in chapter 1, I would draw upon finding peace among chaos and confusion. Sometimes the lesson is that it's time to move on. If you are doing your best work, you do not have to stay in a place where you are not respected and valued.

These strategies worked well for me. I could either allow these situations to defeat me or make me stronger, and I chose the latter. Oftentimes opportunities lead to other opportunities. The connections you make when you put yourself in the position to be "graced" will serve you well later. Professional development opportunities are another way to put yourself in the position to be graced. Such was the case with Marian Wright Edelman and the Children's Defense Fund. Edelman, founder and president of the Children's Defense Fund, wrote two of the most used books in my collection. I often turned to *The Measure of Our Success: A Letter to My Children and Yours* (1992) and *Guide My Feet: Prayers and Meditations on Loving and Working for Children* (1995) in times of contemplation or when I needed the appropriate words of encouragement for staff and families. I still use them today when times are challenging and I need to focus.

In 2000 I applied for and received notice that I'd been selected as a fellow at the Children's Defense Fund Policy and Advocacy Institute for Early Education Leaders. I was ecstatic. I had the awesome opportunity to spend time on the Alex Haley Farm and network with and learn from other emerging early childhood leaders from around the country. Being in that environment at the institute on the Haley Farm was especially meaningful to me as an African American woman. The opportunity to participate in a professional learning experience hosted by a nationally recognized early childhood advocacy organization led by an African American woman on the former homeplace land of the author of *Roots*, the groundbreaking story of an enslaved family and their search to find their African roots, was almost too much for me to believe. One evening the minister of the institute allowed the three women of color who were there to go inside the Haley house (which was off-limits) for a brief moment, and I must admit to being emotionally overwhelmed as I stood in the den where I imagined *Roots* had been penned.

This experience with the institute was moving both emotionally and professionally. I was also able to "be quiet," think about my journey, and consider all the information we were receiving at the institute and the next steps in my career. It was while there that I decided to apply for the position of director of the Wisconsin Early Childhood Association (WECA), the local NAEYC affiliate, for which I had been approached and encouraged to apply.

Two of the people I met while participating in the institute are still my colleagues and friends. Danielle Ewen, now senior policy advisor at Education Counsel, was one of the facilitators of the institute, and Rachel Schumacher, director of the Children's Initiative at the J.B. and M.K. Pritzker Foundation, was my roommate. Danielle and I reconnected when I was a candidate for the NAEYC Governing Board in 2013. Danielle was then a current NAEYC Governing Board member and chair of the nominations committee. She waited for the appropriate time and asked if I remembered her, to which I responded, "Of course I do." All three of us, Danielle, Rachel, and I, had the opportunity to be together again in 2016 when NAEYC had a reception to thank the early childhood staff members of the Obama administration for their work in moving early childhood education forward as a national agenda. Both Danielle and Rachel, who was then the director of the Office of Child Care in the Administration for Children and Families, attended the event, and we had a nice photo op fifteen years in the making!

Sometimes life and career circumstances come full circle. Putting yourself in a position where opportunities can find you and then seizing them when they come along will serve you well on your leadership journey. When I think about the female professionals in this chapter, I recognize that in some way, I reconnected with each of them later in my career. However, at the time of my meeting them, I never thought that our paths would cross again. Who are you becoming acquainted with now that might circle back to you later in your life? Will these people possibly have an impact on your career later on? What will be their remembrance of you and your work? Are you making a good impression on them?

Your Vision

> *One day Alice came to a fork in the road*
>
> *and saw a Cheshire cat in a tree. "Which*
>
> *road do I take?" she asked. His response*
>
> *was a question: "Where do you want*
>
> *to go?" "I don't know," Alice answered.*
>
> *"Then," said the cat, "it doesn't matter."*
>
> *—Lewis Carroll,* Alice's
>
> Adventures in Wonderland

To put yourself in the position of receiving great opportunities in leadership, you need to have a vision of where you want to go. This passage from *Alice's Adventures in Wonderland* by Lewis Carroll points out the importance of having that vision. If you don't know your ultimate destination, you don't know what steps you need to take to get there. What is the vision you have for yourself? I enjoy quotes and have often created vision boards for myself. (See the end of this book for an example of a vision board.) I use them to help me stay focused and aligned with my vision and goals. One of my favorite quotes from my vision boards is "Little girls with dreams grow up to be women with vision."

I think that people like working with and for visionaries, and I know that I do. Their energy and vision are contagious. Visionary leaders are often called innovative; they create a climate and environment in which colleagues and staff members aren't afraid to take risks and, in fact, are usually encouraged to do so. People in leadership positions that can't "see the forest for the trees" are not leaders. They are managers that are, more often than not, caught up in the day to day rather than the big picture and the possibilities. And the people they work with are likely to be overmanaged and underled.

Having a vision of where you want to go doesn't mean that you can't change or adjust it as you move forward in your career. Early in my career, my vision was to own and operate my own child care center. I was going to take all that I had learned and experienced as a teacher and open one of the best, if not the best, child care programs in Milwaukee. I even had a name for the program: Best of Care Child Care Center. However, as my career advanced, I revised the vision I had for myself. I started out in my career journey as a child care assistant teacher and progressed to the roles of teacher, teacher/director, program/center director, child care center licensor, campus children's center administrator, early childhood education adjunct faculty, executive director of the one of the largest child care centers in the state of Wisconsin, and executive director of WECA, the Wisconsin affiliate of NAEYC. I then transitioned to the Milwaukee Public Schools (MPS), where I was hired as the coordinator of a $12 million grant that provided improvement grants and technical assistance to child care centers that then partnered those programs with a district elementary school. At MPS I served as the coordinator of that program and then went on to serve as director of early childhood education and director of innovation. I then began what some may think is a new career path as the executive director of the Milwaukee Public Schools Foundation Inc. However, I'm just being fluid and am still using the same work ethic, big-picture thinking, and relationship building in this new position.

A Builder

Sometimes others can make assessments of your experiences and talents to help you identify a skill set that you may take for granted. These assessments may influence your vision. During my years as the coordinator of early childhood at the MATC, an emerging strength of mine was identified not by me but by those that had recruited me to apply for that position. This strength was described by a recruiter who was interviewing me for a position. She called me "a builder" of programs and people, in reference to the mentoring of emerging leaders and transforming programs work that I was doing. I had not thought of or used the term *builder* for the work I was doing until that day when the recruiter called out the builder in me.

I would eventually identify a component of this quality as "systems thinking": having a mind for the details with the ability to see the big picture as well, being gifted at problem solving, and able to see how all these details interact. Starting at MATC and all the positions that followed, I was responsible for building or rebuilding, reorganizing, rebranding, or reconstituting programs and organizations. Often this was challenging because the folks in these organizations didn't want to change. They were comfortable with the status quo. Change was often a perceived threat to their power. I was challenged in each of those positions, usually by staff members and sometimes by individual board members.

Sometimes the pushback came from the community, which is what happened during the transition of the St. Joseph Day Care Center to the Child Development Center of St. Joseph. The former child care center had been run by nuns, the Felician Sisters of St. Joseph, for over thirty years. The program had transitioned from an orphanage to a child care center. However, the program was vastly out of date and sometimes out of compliance, and the sisters were aging. In 1998 I was able to implement new policies and procedures, staffing structure, and salary scales and move the program into a newly renovated former school building. But not everyone in the community was comfortable with the changes being made. One day I observed the following interaction right outside of my office. A visitor, a man who lived in the neighborhood and had a long-standing relationship with the sisters, came into the building and proclaimed to the sisters that were standing by the entrance, "I hear that you have a new person in charge, and she's not a sister or a Catholic." The sisters, who were not ones for confrontation for the most part, smiled uncomfortably and said hello. I quietly exited my office, walked up to the visitor, and extended my hand, saying, "Hi, I'm Ann Terrell, the new director. Welcome to the center. Is there something I can help you with?" He stood there, speechless and somewhat dumbfounded and obviously surprised by my greeting. Then after a brief silence, said that he periodically comes by to see if he can assist the sisters with any chores. I replied that I hoped that we could continue to take advantage of his generosity, said good-bye, and went back to my office.

As a leader, you must also be an effective communicator. Your actions and words must convey consistency, trust, transparency, ethical behavior, expectations, and vision. In situations where leaders are tested, they will need a strong foundation on which to stand. What are effective leadership communication skills? I have found success in the philosophy that an effective leader acknowledges through her communication that she doesn't have all the answers, but she builds a strong team of people who bring to the table diverse perspectives, experiences, and expertise. She asks smart questions of the team and allows them to problem solve and be critical thinkers for solutions. Another communication strategy that I like to use is telling stories, showing positive ways to deal with problems.

Doing this building work has often provided me with the opportunity to engage in conversations about race and diversity in situations where those conversations had not previously occurred. The MATC downtown campus children's center staff had a reputation for being challenging, and, in fact, the college had a hard time retaining leadership for the program. Several of the faculty members encouraged me to apply, saying to me that they believed that I could make a difference in the program. On my first day of work at the MATC program, the staff had positioned a welcome banner across the top of the door at the entry to the center. The banner read, "Welcome Miss Ann." I was pleased with this sign of promising relationships to come. However, later that morning when I thanked the staff for the sign, I also quietly let them know that the term *Miss Ann* was a bit offensive to me because that was the term that enslaved people called other enslaved people that were perceived as being better than the others. It's the old house-slave, field-slave dialogue. While I suspect that some of the staff knew this bit of history, I remember the look of shock on the face of one staff member in particular as she apologized. When they then asked what the children would call me, I said, "They can call me 'Ann' or 'Ms. Terrell,' whichever they are developmentally able to artic-ulate." Some of the staff strongly objected to this, indicating that the chil-dren would not respect me if I allowed them to call me by my first name, to which I responded that it's not what they called me that would determine the respect; it's the relationship I fostered with them that would. The banner was down by 10:00 a.m., probably removed by one of the staff during a morning break. I don't know because I didn't ask; I never brought up the subject again. That day I established myself as the leader of the program and shared my expectations for how we all would interact with the children in our care.

At the time, though we were a campus-based early childhood program, we not only enrolled children of students, faculty, and staff but also children from the community, often children of families who were working in the downtown Milwaukee area. Our diverse population included children and families representing different ethnicities, cultures, languages, and socioeco-nomic classes. I believe that because of the strong stance I took that first day, I opened the door for conversations about race and poverty, and how they intersected with the early childhood education and care we were providing. Additionally, as a team, the staff members and I were able to build a cul-ture of respect for one another and the children and families we served. Our definition of *team* was broad and included our maintenance staff as well. Our lead maintenance person was a Latina woman who maintained our center as if it were her own home, not only performing the routine cleaning but daily wiping down every doorknob, light switch, and other common places that the adults and children frequently touched. She came in daily at the begin-ning of her shift as our day was winding down, and she would address the children and staff by name. She invited the children to call her "Jualita," which she explained was interpreted as *grandmother* in some Spanish dialects.

This culture of respect was reinforced about a month later when I had to intervene in a child–parent interaction that occurred during end-of-the-day pickup. I was in my office and overheard a very loud adult voice coming from the coatroom area. The adult was speaking to a child in a very loud, harsh tone. I approached the area and observed someone that I recognized as one of our students' parents trying to put a coat on her child. At this point, she was also physically hitting the child, and the little girl was loudly crying. I'm sure the whole center could hear the interaction, including other parents who were picking up children. I approached the parent and very intently and quietly said to her, "I'm sorry, but I cannot allow you to do that here." The parent looked up at me and said in a combative manner something like, "Oh, so you're going to tell me how to raise my child." By now we were being observed by other center staff members, and I realized that this was an opportunity to send a message to them as well. I needed to quickly assess the situation and deliver a response that would address the situation at hand and meet the parent's and child's needs at the same time. I then responded by quietly saying to the parent, "My name is Ann Terrell and I am the new director here at the center. What I'm saying to you, from one Black woman to another, is that if you continue to hit your child, I will have to report you for child abuse." The parent then stopped her behavior, looked at me, and said, "No one has ever told me that before." I then stooped down to the child's eye level and, while I helped her put on her coat, said to her that her mother had had a very long day and was probably tired and really needed her coopera-tion in getting dressed to go home. I walked both of them to the door, hugged them both and said I'd see them in the morning. I ended the interaction by saying to the parent that I would be available for her if she ever needed to talk.

This interaction was very telling to me in a number of ways. It said to me that this wasn't the first time that type of parent-child interaction had taken place and that there was a dire need for the staff to be supported in under-standing and carrying out their jobs, including cultural competency and communication professional development. I met with individual staff members the next day, and they shared with me that they felt a lack of empowerment and knowledge in how to intervene in those types of situations. And while my relationship with that parent started out somewhat strained, we did develop a mutually respectful relationship. About a year or so later when the parent completed her program at the college, she made the decision to transfer her two children (she'd had another baby daughter during that time) to a community-based child care program. A few weeks later, she came to my office and asked if she could reenroll her children in the center, saying the other program "doesn't love my babies the way y'all do." That statement affirmed for me that what we were doing and the services we were providing to parents and children were successful. Those interactions set the pace for the rebuilding of the MATC program, including staff professionalism and the building of and relocation to a new NAEYC-accredited center where we welcomed then first lady Hillary Rodham Clinton some years later.

As you can see, my work as a builder has been about more than building my own career and relationships with colleagues. Early childhood leaders of programs and classrooms must build intentional, honest, positive, respectful, and real relationships with the parents and children they serve in order for learning to take place for all involved in those relationships. Had I not intervened in an honest and intentional way with that mother, the outcome could have been very different. Perhaps a teacher or another parent would have reported the incident to social services, and the center and the parent would have ended up implicit in the harm of a child.

Challenges Are Opportunities

My early experience working for MPS was interesting and challenging. I encountered many silos and little interest in collaboration from those in charge of other early childhood programs, although many of us were working in the same schools with the same teachers, children, and families, only implementing different programs. I began to share information on "braiding" early childhood funding and the potential for program and student impact with those in administrative leadership positions, including then MPS superintendent William Andrekopoulos. I was also sharing with the superintendent current research on closing the so-called achievement gap with quality early childhood education programming.

There were several times that my work was brought to the attention of the superintendent. Once was by an organization held in high regard and esteem by the community that I, in my role as coordinator of the Community and Child Care Partnership program, had refused to provide reimbursement for some charges they indicated they had incurred while carrying out their role in our project. I believed that there was clear evidence of duplication of receipts and invoices and did not approve the reimbursement. The director of the organization called the superintendent to complain, and a meeting was held. I clearly presented my documentation of the duplication, and my decision not to reimburse was upheld. Another instance was when the district's external auditors told the superintendent that they had never before seen in the district record keeping as excellent as mine.

It was about this time when Superintendent Andrekopoulos asked me to take on the leadership of the district's Head Start program. The program had faced some significant challenges in meeting compliance with Head Start policy standards and regulations. My experience told me this was due in part to a lack of administrative and program experience by those in charge. I discovered that there was also a lack of understanding of how to implement the Head Start standards and that there was a complete lack of the necessary systems in place needed for the implementation of a successful Head Start program. I took on the charge I was given, and within a year's time, the program received a certificate of compliance from the federal office. It wasn't easy. Some staff members were terminated, and others were given the opportunity to fill other positions, while some just made the decision to retire. There was also a lot of professional development for all the Head Start teachers and family partnership coordinators. The principals of the buildings where the Head Start program was housed and the school board members were also included in professional development opportunities and the overhaul of the program. Family members were informed about the significant role they played in the administration of the Head Start program, and I held family meetings and offered the families classes and other opportunities to further encourage their involvement. I didn't do this alone. The superintendent brought in retired MPS principal Dorothy St. Charles to assist me with this work, and we contracted with Mable Jones of The Jones Connection, from Atlanta, Georgia, for much of the training and professional development.

One day during budget season, Superintendent Andrekopoulos called me to his office and asked me what an MPS division of early childhood education would be composed of: what the vision, mission, and goals of such a department would be. I asked him when he'd like to have the document, and he said in one week. I actually had it for him within three days because I had already given this matter some comprehensive thought. I had been thinking ahead, and I was ready to present my ideas. I presented him with a comprehensive white paper that included a vision and some initial goals for the new department, outlined which programs should be housed within the new division, and included the current research to support this new division. The new division was included as part of a reorganization plan adopted with the new school budget by the board of school directors and became effective in July 2005. The division included the MPS Head Start and HighScope programs, the Curriculum Materials Development Center (an early childhood professional development center) and Wisconsin's Student Achievement Guarantee in Education (SAGE) early childhood classroom size reduction programs, the early childhood community-based contracted K4 classroom sites, and Reading First and Early Reading First grants.

> *"Hard times require furious dancing."*
>
> *—African proverb*

My leadership journey has taken many different paths, all leading to where I am now. At points in my career, especially those that had been particularly challenging, I often asked myself, "Why?" or "Why me?" I was doing the right thing by the children and people I was working for, so why were there so many challenges? Finally it dawned on me that those challenging times were preparing me for the next step in my career, moving me along the pathway to my next destination. I was putting myself in a good position for what was coming next.

Sometimes personal challenges and problems are your spirit encouraging you to make changes. You don't feel "balanced" and in tune with yourself. Growth requires change, and it is during these challenging times that we must examine what life is trying to tell us to reorganize. There is a saying that when one door closes, another opens up. I don't think of those opportunities as doors closing; I have tried to take the lessons I learned in each of my career "steps" and move on to the next phase. "Just keeping it moving," as my friend and colleague Vincent Costanza said when I congratulated him on a special career move. "I learned a lot about grace and class from you," he added.

Regardless of what kind of leader you aspire to be, be ready when your opportunity comes. It may be unexpected. Stay informed of what's happening in your field and stay on top of the current research, areas of focus, and discussion. Someone may recognize leadership potential in you that you have not recognized in yourself. Be ready for the ball when it's passed to you and position yourself to take the shot.

The first time I was asked to serve on a panel and share my expert opinion was at a statewide symposium on infant and toddler care. I contemplated heavily about whether or not to accept this offer because it was the first time I'd be speaking publicly as an "expert" panel member, and I wasn't exactly comfortable speaking before large audiences. I don't remember the exact situation that led up to the invitation; however, it was because someone had heard me speak about infant and toddler care elsewhere. I was one of the first people in Milwaukee, probably in all of Wisconsin, to receive the approved training and be certified to provide child care for children under two years of age. Based on my experience in the classroom and leading programs, I felt strongly that providing high-quality infant and toddler care was critical for children labeled "at risk," and I was very vocal about my concern.

So after much reflection, I accepted the invitation to speak. I wrote out my talking points and thoughts and served on the panel. The event led to more speaking engagements and leadership opportunities at the local and state level. You see, I realized I was either going to be at the table or on the menu, so to speak. Shirley Chisholm, the first African American and the first woman to run for US president, once said, "If they don't give you a seat at the table, bring a folding chair" (Pierre 2016). I was either going to be an influencer or be on the receiving end of the decision-making process. I made a conscious decision to be a person who influences. Don't be intimidated or discouraged if there's no one at the table that looks like you. You've earned the right to be there. Keep doing your work and remember to bring others along with you.

"Your time as a caterpillar has expired

and your wings are ready!"

—*Donna Pisani*

CHAPTER 3

Leadership Is Service

"Leaders are visionaries with a poorly developed sense of fear and no concept of the odds against them."

—*Robert Jarvik*

What kind of leader are you now? What kind of leader do you want to be? I knew what kind of leader I wanted to be based on the people I had the privilege to work for. Each one of them taught me something about leadership, leading teams and organizations, and I value the lessons I gleaned from them. Whether the lesson was on how to promote or acknowledge a job well done, how to provide job performance feedback to a staff member, or how to create a high-performing team, I was a keen observer of the leadership styles that made them successful.

In their *Harvard Business Review* article "Seven Transformations of Leadership," David Rooke and William R. Torbert (2005) describe these seven types of leaders:

- **OPPORTUNIST:** wins by any means possible; self-oriented; manipulative

- **DIPLOMAT:** avoids overt conflict; wants to belong; helps bring people together

- **EXPERT:** rules by logic and expertise; seeks rational efficiency

- **ACHIEVER:** meets strategic goals; effectively achieves goals through teams

- **INDIVIDUALIST:** interweaves competing personal and company action logics

- **STRATEGIST:** exercises the power of mutual inquiry, vigilance, and vulnerability

- **ALCHEMIST:** integrates material, spiritual, and societal transformation

If we look at each of those types of leaders individually, I imagine the opportunist is the most challenging type to work with and for. For the opportunist, the work isn't about the good of the organization or its customers, only about the leader. In avoiding overt conflict, the diplomat may fail to confront internal or external factors that detract from the organization or its work to move forward, for example, racism or sexism in the workplace. The expert leader reminds me of *Star Trek*'s Mr. Spock: always rational. However, we are human beings, not the fictional Vulcans, and sometimes we make mistakes and must find ways of regrouping and moving forward. Personally, I would like to work for and with someone who is a combination of the list above.

While this is not meant to be a comprehensive list of ways people lead, it does provide a good outline of the different types of leaders we may be or leaders we have worked with. Do you see yourself in the list above? I see myself in several of the types; perhaps depending on the situation, I can be a diplomatic leader or an achiever. There are times when I have been an individualist or could have been described as an alchemist. The best leaders take into account the situations at hand and the people on the team to determine how to lead. You might not use the same strategy in a large meeting as you would in a one-on-one, or you might not work with one staff member the same as you would with another because you are recognizing their strengths and challenges. Just as we individualize curriculum and lesson plans to meet the needs of young children, leaders are called upon to analyze situations and people and determine how to lead in each unique instance.

Leadership and management are not the same. Leadership requires a vision for the future. Management does not; it is about control of the day to day. A good leader knows when to use and how to balance both of these strategies, as they are not interchangeable. Stephen R. Covey, A. Roger Merrill, and Rebecca R. Merrill say, "Management works within the system. Leadership works on the system" (1994, 27). Leaders are also change agents. They inspire and motivate their teams to get the most out of them. But first, they must establish credibility with the team.

How does a person in a leadership role establish her credibility as a leader? The characteristics of integrity, honesty, trust, and humilty are all key to establishing yourself as a credible leader. It's my experience that staff members, much like the children in our classrooms who observe their teachers, observe and listen to their leaders very carefully to find out who they really are—what they truly are about. Leaders cannot waffle on their decisions and actions or play favorites. They must be true to their word and operate with integrity and a set of moral standards, demonstrating responsibility for their actions. Some years ago, my cousin Martha—or Dot, as the family calls her—shared with me a tip to be "fair, firm, and friendly." She drew a distinction between being friends in the workplace and being friendly. If a leader acts and performs consistently, the team learns to trust the leader and will perform with the same dedication and integrity as the leader.

A Team Environment

A team is a group of individuals with a common goal. Successful teams have a meaningful common purpose that is identified at the beginning of their work together, or it is formed during their work together along with their goals and objectives. A smart leader will bring to the table people with a diverse set of skills and knowledge to form a team. I always shared with my team members that they were chosen because they had knowledge or an expertise that I didn't have. By using this form of collective leadership, my goal was to have a team that was well rounded and that we could all be proud to be a part of. We operated from a place of belief that displaying partnership with, trust in, and responsibility to one another would have a much greater impact than if we operated in silos.

Another aspect of leadership is making connections and building relationships. It is said that all learning is understanding relationships; this is true in teamwork as well. The leader must be a keen observer of the team, both as individuals and in group settings, in order to identify each person's individual strengths and build upon these strengths as team members. The leader builds upon the individual team member's strengths, helping them fulfill their potential and thereby motivating them to be successful individuals and team players. The leader facilitates the building of these relationships and inspires the team members, not necessarily by their words but by their actions.

Are you responsible for leading a team? Have you formed a common objective and identified one another's strengths? Are various team members allowed to lead the team depending on the work at hand and their skill set or expertise? Have you built trust with one another yet? What is your plan for building your team?

Early in my tenure as the director of early childhood education for the Milwaukee Public Schools (MPS), one of the first items of business was strategic planning for the newly formed team. I brought in professional facilitators, and the process included our internal and community partners as well. The facilitators made notes about the behavior of the team members. Some of the team members displaying certain behaviors were labeled as *blocker*, *withdrawer*, or *destroyer*. These behaviors were exhibited by people who believed they should've been named the head of our department, so they were determined to be combative and uncooperative throughout the process. Eventually our community members called out the behavior, and we were able to move the strategic planning forward and create vision and mission statements and guiding principles for our work together. Our team began the practice of placing our mission statement on the reverse side of our business cards as a way of proclaiming it and living it out loud. Everyone needs to have a vision for the future. If you want to improve staff performance, understanding what the vision is and regularly articulating it to and with the team will help to give the team purpose. How often do you articulate your vision to your team and others?

During my time as director, I was leading a team of staff members who were responsible for the district's HighScope and Head Start programs, Reading First and Early Reading First grants, SAGE early childhood classroom size reduction programs and P5, and the community's contracted early childhood programs. At one point, the literacy and library media offices were part of our team. One of my former colleagues once asked me how I was able to establish such a high-performing team. Our supervisor was in earshot of the question and responded that I'd been able to build my own team. While I had indeed been able to hire and put in place several members of our staff of nine, I had inherited most of our team members. But when the opportunity to hire presented itself, I brought people to the table who had expertise or experience in an area that the rest of the team, myself included, did not. Again, I strived for a well-rounded leadership team. I was also able to model the expectations I had of the staff. I was part of the team, and they understood that I was firm but fair. I set the bar and the standard of expectation for performance. We had clear goals and deadlines, and I encouraged feedback. People who worked with us were always surprised by our ability to promptly respond to requests for information. We had established a culture of collaboration on our team, and we had created an environment where things got done. Staff members were comfortable going to each other to problem solve or work together on a project without me asking or directing them to. I didn't micromanage, but I did hold the team accountable. When there was a problem, we solved it together—all voices were heard and respected at the table.

When we had staff meetings, I invited other district staff and community members that touched the work we did in an effort to break down some of the silos that existed at the time. This aspect of our collective leadership, bringing to the table other district staff and community members who impacted our work, required a shift in thinking for some of the staff. For example, the district had created a set of standards, called Learning Targets, for the K5–12 students. But they hadn't created these standards for the four-year-olds who were served by the district, so our department took the lead in that work. To the surprise and chagrin of some staff members, I brought in representatives of the other Head Start grantee agencies, the local child care resource and referral agency, and early childhood faculty and trainers. Collaboratively we created standards not only for the four-year-olds in the district but also for those served in community-based settings as well. And for the first time, these district standards also included targets for the social and emotional learning of the students.

Collaboration was an important component to the success of the teams that I worked with and led. I've heard it said before that true collaboration requires that the participants give up something when they come to the table. I'm not quite sure I fully embrace that concept, but I do know that successful collaboration incorporates and honors diversity of people, ideas, perspectives, and experiences. Some characteristics of successful collaboration are intentional talking and listening, openness, fairness, and respect. This type of collaboration produces shared ownership and builds the team's capacity for higher performance.

How do you accomplish successful collaborative relationships, especially where relationships have not been established in the past, except for perhaps individual working relationships? What is the value of collaborations?

Successful collaborative efforts incorporate a diversity of folks at the table along with their ideas, perspectives, and experiences. The participants must have a set of agreed-upon standards to operate by, including commitment, respect, openness, listening and talking, and fairness. All parties at the table are considered equal, agree to be fully present, and will have the opportunity to equally participate. Collaboration also requires a set of shared goals, and, if these are in place, the outcome will be of greater value than would have been realized by the individuals or organizations working in silos. Additionally, based on my experience in these types of efforts, collaboration brings about an extension of the community, new partners and alliances to engage with, and shared understanding of the participants and ownership of the solutions.

> *"Many hands make light work."*
>
> *—Tanzanian proverb*

As the director of early childhood education for MPS, I also created the opportunity for team building and getting to know one another outside of the office. One day in early spring, after work, we all met at a furrier and tried on fur coats. While none of us made a purchase that day, we had fun with one another. One year during Christmas break, I had the team over to my house for dinner and fellowship. I cooked the dinner and presented each team member with a present from me. The relationships I established with the team went beyond the professional to the personal; they often felt comfortable enough to come to me with their personal issues—not to solve the problems, just to listen and allow them the opportunity to reflect. During the celebration of one of my milestone birthdays, the team and my other mentees stood and gave testimony to my mentoring. I was deeply touched as they shared with those present how I had mentored them. Kortney Smith, formerly the director of the MPS Head Start program and now principal of an elementary school in Brown Deer, Wisconsin, said, "Not only did I speak with Ann about my professional challenges, I also shared with her about my personal struggles as well."

How do great leaders inspire their teams? Do they walk the talk and, as previously discussed, help staff believe they work for a winner? How is this accomplished? How do successful leaders communicate? Clear communication, verbal and nonverbal, is essential to leadership. Bringing your vision to life and communicating that vision in ways that will reach the team members is key. However, just as we differentiate learning for students, we must also keep in mind that adults receive information in a variety of ways.

Always having a meeting agenda is step one. Whether it's a meeting for one or twenty-one, the reason for meeting needs to be clear. I like to tell stories to help get my point across, and I also believe that it helps build relationships with the staff when you present your more personal side. The leader should also be mindful of what she doesn't know and be up front and honest about it with the staff. This will assist in building a trusting climate for staff members and will allow them to be open to engaging in conversations and meetings. It also adds to the can-do attitude of a high-performing team.

Dr. Tanya Johnson, who worked with me at MPS as one of the program directors, said of my leadership style, "Under your leadership, you modeled skills that are needed to be an effective early childhood leader: build relationships, work with integrity, stay abreast of current early childhood issues, validate your actions with research, be an advocate for young children, and be culturally relevant. Those six skills have been my leadership compass. I have embedded each one into my leadership practice and use them to stand in my truth when educators lose sight of the value of early childhood."

Use Your Gifts: Servant Leadership

> *"How can you sing of amazing grace and all God's wonders without using your hands?"*
>
> *—Mahalia Jackson*

I am a strong believer in the practice of servant leadership. My family members were examples of servant leadership for me throughout my life and also in my leadership roles throughout my career. I've drawn on their examples of giving back to the community through educational leadership.

To practice servant leadership, one generally has to embrace a philosophy of enriching their organizations and communities. Leading with honesty and integrity while putting children first was modeled for me by the women that raised me and lifted up the ideal of educational opportunities for others, either by teaching or leading educational efforts in the community. In 2008 I received the Black Women's Network Legacy of Leadership in Education Award. The master of ceremonies noted during my introduction that "she serves and serves and serves" in reference to the community boards, committees, and councils that I was participating in.

Servant leadership can be displayed through day-to-day actions and interactions. In her book *One Day My Soul Just Opened Up*, Iyanla Vanzant writes:

> Let me Remember
> To SERVE is an act of love.
> My SERVICE is a divine gift to the world.
> When I do what I love, I am richly rewarded.
> Service and poverty do not coexist.
> Passion+Focus+Purpose=SERVICE
> When I give SERVICE, survival is guaranteed. (1998, 180)

Servant leadership is a philosophy of service first. The servant-leader shares power and focuses on the development of those she works with as well as those she serves. The desired outcome is the wholeness of the people and the community and that those served will, in turn, also serve and build a stronger community. This is a goal I hoped to accomplish as I led different teams throughout my career and mentored emerging leaders.

Servant-leaders often lead from a place of purpose and passion; again, service is the priority, not the leadership position. According to Robert Greenleaf, there are generally ten characteristics of servant-leaders. I think these fit well within the definition of graceful leadership.

LISTENING

The servant-leader is committed to listening to people and communities. This commitment to the community is played out by asking who's not at the table—whose voice is not being heard. The commitment to listen is also to listen to oneself, that honest self-reflection that all leaders must have the ability to embrace, and then building upon that honest self-reflection with personal growth and change.

EMPATHY

The servant-leader is not only committed to listening to others but also to empathizing with them. This reminds me of the "walking a mile in their shoes" adage. When I hear my typically white, middle-income colleagues compare themselves and their status to others by saying that they made it all on their own, by studying and working hard, and they don't understand why others can't do the same, I must remind them that they are dismissing 265 years of enslavement and almost 100 years of segregation, lynching, and Jim Crow. Black folks in this country have been "free" for only 50 years, less than my lifetime. Let's think about empathy and understanding with these facts in mind.

AWARENESS

Related to empathy is the characteristic of self-awareness and, I would say, awareness in general, as servant-leaders strive to see a bigger, more holistic picture of situations. They are good observers of their environment and demonstrate systems thinking at its best.

HEALING

Servant leadership offers opportunity for healing of relationships. Servant-leaders encourage and support the personal growth of individuals on their team or in the group. When a servant-leader recognizes talent in emerging leaders, she promotes and supports these people rather than seeing them as a threat, as often happens. Sometimes when we offer the opportunity for healing and a new start, the person on the receiving end doesn't have the same vision as you do. I begin relationships with trust and will continue that relationship until that trust is broken. And even then, I try to reject the behavior and not the person. However, I'm also cognizant of the advice from Dr. Maya Angelou that "when people show you who they are, believe them . . . the first time" (quoted in Winfrey 2011). I have found that some colleagues and coworkers do not understand how I'm able to extend this grace. I actually had one former staff member ask me why she was given another chance because she had violated my trust when she deliberately misrepresented the truth to members of another department in regard to a document she submitted to them, saying that I had reviewed it when in fact I had not. She not only jeopardized her reputation but also the job performance of the person she worked with in the other department, as her supervisor called her to task on the matter. The relationship between me and this staff member was never the same, and she eventually transferred into another position, telling people she didn't know why I was treating her differently, not acknowledging the role she played in creating the distance. I could no longer trust her, and trust is vital to me in the working relationships I have with people.

PERSUASION

Servant-leaders are not power wielders; they are able to build consensus within groups. In 2004 I was appointed by then Wisconsin governor Jim Doyle as chair of the Quality Counts early childhood task force. I was very pleased with the fact that I was able to lead this group of twenty-four diverse early childhood leaders from all over the state of Wisconsin to consensus on the recommendations brought forward for the creation of the Wisconsin child care quality rating system, which has evolved to YoungStar.

STEWARDSHIP

Closely related to consensus building and persuasion is stewardship. Building or establishing trust is important in both of these leadership characteristics. In the case of stewardship, the trust is about the commitment to the greater good.

FORESIGHT

Foresight, what some call *intuition*, allows the leader to learn from the past, understand the present, and think about the consequences of the future.

CONCEPTUALIZATION

Servant-leaders are visionary and often have to work hard to balance the art of conceptual thinking with the day-to-day focus. They set goals for themselves, for their teams and team members, and for their organization. These servant-leaders have to be very organized individuals in order to balance conceptual thinking and day-to-day management, and they must practice patience.

This characteristic is especially challenging for me. Quite often in my career, I've been able to visualize the outcomes of innovative changes and have wanted to see those changes occur right away. However, working within systems to make changes can oftentimes be a slow process and can sometimes be quite frustrating for servant-leaders.

COMMITMENT TO THE GROWTH OF PEOPLE AND BUILDING COMMUNITY

The last two characteristics are closely joined: the commitment to the growth of people, and the building of community. These two are especially important to me. I take very seriously the responsibility for the growth of the people I work with and to build a community for and with them. The best example of this was my tenure as the director of early childhood education for MPS. During that time, we had a team built on trust and commitment to the students we served. We went through strategic planning and created vision and mission statements and guiding principles for our work together. When there were new members of the team, we reviewed these principles to determine if they were still relevant or needed revising. I believe the team members knew I cared for each of them individually and as a group and trusted them to do what we were charged with doing. Of course, there were instances of people not being a good fit for our team, not having enough experience, or not understanding our form of leadership, but overall we became known for being a high-performing, innovative team. Each of the women I worked with then have become great leaders in their own right. Many of them are currently leading organizations, schools, and early childhood community-based programs.

> *"I do not at all understand the mystery of grace—only that it meets us where we are but does not leave us where it found us."*
>
> —*Anne Lamott,* Traveling Mercies: Some Thoughts on Faith

Real Leaders

I believe that a leader is someone that can influence the decisions and actions of others. However, I also have to acknowledge that some people use this influence and power negatively, either deliberately or due to lack of experience in a leadership role. Real leaders seek out opportunities to challenge the status quo in meaningful and productive ways, leading by example and then inspiring, enabling, and empowering others to act for the betterment or good of their community or organization. True leaders understand that it is not about themselves but about the legacy they will leave for others, and, almost as important, good leaders know when and how to follow.

Leadership is not about position on an organizational chart. Leadership takes place wherever and whenever someone makes decisions that will impact others. Leaders are not only directors, administrators, or principals. There are many teacher-leaders in classrooms across the country. Teachers who, each and every school day, make decisions on curriculum and instruction that will touch the lives of children. Teachers whose words and acknowledgements can either hurt or heal. These classroom environments and materials have a tremendous impact on students that may not be realized for years to come.

CHAPTER 4

Who Are You?

"My mother, she was my first friend in

the proper sense of the word. She was not

an emotional person, she was completely

controlled, calm, at peace with herself and

the world."

—*Nelson Mandela*

In order to move along the leadership path, I believe you must know who you are as a person at your core, understand what your passion is, and know what grounds you so that you can live and work from a place of purpose. In other words, you must know what it is you stand for, what values you will absolutely stand upon no matter what. Knowing who you are and whose you are is imperative in leadership positions. You must be able to define yourself and speak for yourself in order to lead; you must know yourself and understand your value.

In 1993 the theme of my family reunion on the paternal side of the family was *sankofa*. *Sankofa* is a Ghanaian word that translates to "Go back and get it" or "Return and reclaim that which is forgotten." The symbol of *sankofa* is a bird, the body of which is facing forward while the head is looking back. I love this symbol as a representation of the leadership journey. Its very representation means that you can't move forward without understanding the past, knowing who you are, whose you are, and what you believe in. That old saying is true: if you do not understand your past, you're doomed to repeat it or not move forward.

The following Facebook post was made in 2012, during a celebration of teachers: "My first teacher surrounded me with the *African American Children's Bible, Jambo Means Hello, The Story of Kwanzaa,* and *Spin a Soft Black Song* by Nikki Giovanni. . . . Thus making it impossible that I wouldn't have a love for literature and a love for Black people across the globe. Thank you, Mom, for the years of attention & intention you gave to shaping who I am. I love you." That post was made by my older daughter Jenise; my younger daughter Kenisha shared it with me because she knew I would want to see it but would probably not because I had not joined Facebook at that time. I'm proud that I've always tried to instill a deep appreciation for African American history and culture in my children and now my grandchildren. I hope that this understanding of who we are and whose we are serves them well as a beacon in guiding them through their lives.

"Our family is filled with hope and faith;

held together with love and grace."

—author unknown

"Who yo' people is?" is a question Black folks used to ask each other, especially when a couple started dating. It probably came about as a result of the history of African people in this country and the institution of slavery when families were split up and family members were often sold off. There were not accurate written records available to these enslaved or formerly enslaved people, and so as a way of assuring there were not cousins marrying cousins, the question was asked. When I facilitate a class or workshop on cultural diversity or cultural competence, I often will ask the participants to introduce themselves by telling the "story" of their name. So let me introduce myself to you via the history of my name and the leadership lessons I learned from the people who raised me. My ancestors and elders are people who, by their words or actions, passed on lessons that I have been wise enough to listen to and learn from.

Truth Matters

As I began to write this book, I had heard and believed one version of my family history, and halfway through writing it, I discovered another chapter of my family history that smacked me right in the face. As an African American woman, I understand our history in this country and have always understood that there were probably slave–slaveholder relationships in my family, as both sides of my family were very light-skinned Black people. However, I have had a couple of recent experiences that unsettled me, and I came face-to-face with the painful truth of the maternal side of my family.

Ancestry.com offered their DNA test at a reduced price for Christmas sales, and I purchased one. I was hoping to find out where in Africa my roots were. I spit in the tube, sent off the test, and waited for what seemed like months. Finally the email came that my results were ready. I went online and was happy to discover that I am 67 percent African, mostly Ghanaian and Nigerian. However, I was surprised to find out, or have it confirmed, that I have 32 percent European ancestry, with 28 percent of that being from Great Britain. When my cousin Martha Dorsey used to talk about how she wanted to do the DNA test to find out where in Africa we were from, I used to jokingly tell her that she should know that it would be traced back to Europe somewhere, given the family's oral history and looks. However, I was not prepared for 32 percent!

Ancestry.com also connects you to people you could possibly be related to based on your test results. One of my connections was to the family of Sonja Pierce. She and I connected, and it turns out I'm related to her husband and his side of the family, the Bells. Sonja and I communicated via email and phone, and in person one day when I was in Chicago. Sonja had been researching her husband's family tree for years. She shared with me pictures of relatives I had not seen before, including one of Caleb Bell, who turned out to be the slave owner that impregnated my great-great-great-grandmother, Isabella Leavell, his slave. This relationship produced Luther Bell, my great-great-grandfather. It is one thing to intellectually know of your ancestor's pain, but to come face-to-face with the truth takes an emotional toll on your soul. I started to realize that I really didn't know who I was. However, does this change who I am fundamentally?

My given name is Ann McClain Terrell. I always believed that Ann is after my paternal great-grandmother, Annie Bell Terrell, affectionately known as "Little Mama" because she was this petite woman. However, Ann could very well be after Ann McLean (McClain), my maternal great-great-great-grandmother. I was the first grandchild and great-grandchild on my father's side of the family, and so I learned at a very early age that I was special, though not spoiled. The people on my father's side of the family tree were farmers of tobacco, chickens, and hogs.

My middle name, McClain, comes from my maternal side of the family. (Census takers often made mistakes in the recording of names, and the 1880 census has my great-great-great-grandfather listed as McLean.) Jeremiah McLean was a Cherokee Indian on the Trail of Tears. One of the Trail of Tears stops was Guthrie, Kentucky, close to my birthplace of Allensville, Kentucky, and the small town where I spent part of my early years, Elkton, Kentucky. Jeremiah, for an unknown reason, was not made to travel on to Oklahoma. He made his home in Elkton, Kentucky. Jeremiah ("Jerry McLean" in the written records I've been able to find) was married to Ann McLean, and they were the parents of Underwood McClain, who was the father of Lee McClain and grandfather of Mayme Lee McClain. Mayme Lee McClain married Virgil Small, and they became the parents of two children, my Aunt Betsy and my mother, Patricia Jane Small. When I was born, there hadn't been a boy born on that side of the family in almost sixty years, since Lee. The family wanted to make sure the name was carried on, and so it became my middle name.

Education Is in My Blood

For all of my young life, I understood that my maternal grandmother, Mayme Lee McClain-Small (known as "Mama Mayme"), was involved in the educational life of my small hometown. When she was a young girl growing up in small-town Elkton, Black girls, or any other Black folk for that matter, typically didn't go to school past the eighth grade. However, my grandmother was graced with the opportunity to attend CME High School in Jackson, Tennessee, for her high school completion. The Colored (now Christian) Methodist Episcopal Church was founded with a priority to establish schools for the newly freed, formerly enslaved, Negroes of the South following the Civil War. In 1882 they founded the CME High School. In 1896 the high school officially became Lane College, with a goal of preparing "preachers and teachers." Lee McClain and other ancestors were some of the founding members and were involved in the building and the establishment of Phillips Chapel, our local CME church. So it was fitting that my grandmother would have the opportunity to attend CME High School. After completing high school, she continued on with her enrollment in Lane College and received a "normal school" teaching license in about 1926. When she returned home to Elkton, she became the first Black woman to teach in the all-white schools. While she was not given a regular teaching assignment, she was hired as a long-term substitute.

Even after my family decided to move to Milwaukee, I would visit my grandmother in the summer months. I vividly remember her going to meetings and being involved in the education system. She obviously had no school-age children when I was a young girl, but she stayed involved in the education of the community and sent a loud unspoken message about the importance of education, not just for her family but for the community as a whole. I heard and valued her message, and I've tried to carry that message in my work. I've always said that the quality of education I provide or am responsible for providing to other people's children should be of the same quality that I would want for my own.

My mother was a very smart woman and carried on her mother's message on the importance of education in her own way. From 1979 to 1981, I was a student in the early childhood associate degree program at Milwaukee Area Technical College (MATC). It was very interesting being one of the older students—after all, I was already a mother of two girls, five and three years old at this time. One day in my second year, one of the other "older" students, Norma Anwar, asked if I was related to Pat Terrell. I told her yes, that Patricia was my mother. I will never forget her response. She very excitedly said, "That's why you are the way you are about children!" I didn't understand and certainly didn't know that she knew my mother. She went on to explain that when Title I first became law, around 1966, my mother served on the first Milwaukee Public School's Title I parent committee. She said that my mother was the committee member that translated the Title I legislation and policies for the other parents, which was very empowering for the parents. Norma then went on to tell me that when the school board members got wind of this, they ordered my mother to be removed from the committee, interpreting the membership guidelines to mean that only parents who qualified for Title I should be members of the committee. My mother had a well-paying job working for the United States Postal Service, and so we did not meet that qualification. Norma went on to say that by this time, the parent committee had been empowered and filed an appeal to the state Department of Public Instruction, who in turn reversed the Milwaukee School Board decision and ruled that my mother could indeed serve. Now, Patricia Jane was a very proud woman, and she refused to officially return to the committee, but she continued to work with the other parents in an unofficial capacity.

As the oldest of her children, this was the first time I had heard this story. I remembered that my mother seemed to always be at the school or some school meeting, but I never knew why. I really appreciated Norma's sharing this story with me and was again reaffirmed in regard to my family's message that it's not about us but about the betterment of the community. Norma shared, "Your mother was so smart; she was a good teacher and loved people. She was fair, and she made sure that the parents understood their rights."

At my mother's funeral years later in 1990, the principal of the school, Herman Goldberg, and Norma spoke about their respect for my mother and her commitment to education, not only for her children but for the community's children. Mr. Goldberg spoke about her involvement at the school long after she had any children there, just as my grandmother, her mother, had done in Elkton, Kentucky.

My passion for education and teaching has been encouraged and reinforced throughout my life. What encouraged you to embark on this path? Sometimes that influence comes from outside your family. When you look back at your childhood, do you remember a teacher who helped you see how special you are and who affirmed you? Ms. Powell was my first teacher when my family moved from Kentucky to Milwaukee. I was a student at LaFollette Elementary School and remember not being happy about moving to Milwaukee. I remember believing that it was cold, and this new experience of snow was not very welcoming. I thought the houses all looked alike and were so close together! I also remember being teased by the other students because of my good grades, thin body structure, and southern drawl. I was often called the teacher's pet and some other unfriendly names. But Ms. Powell, through her kindness and compassion, helped me adjust to my new home.

Your Background, Your Leadership

What has been your path to educational leadership? As you consider your own ancestry and upbringing, you may notice that a commitment to education has long been a value of your people, or you might be the first one to chart a new career pathway. As you explore your background, you may discover some qualities, characteristics, or skill sets that others in your family also possess, but you are using them in a different way.

Who influenced you in your life and career? What lessons did you learn from them? As you consider your own *sankofa*, how will you move forward while understanding, respecting, and honoring the past?

Your personal identity is as important as your professional identity. Here's an exercise I was introduced to that will help you tell your personal story. It is a template of prompters, questions for you to respond to about your personal memories and reflections. This originated from the Kentucky 2015–2016 poet laureate George Ella Lyon. It was her goal to collect a "Where I'm From" poem for every county in the state of Kentucky. It is now used internationally as a template for others to write their stories. You can learn more here: www .georgeellalyon.com and www.artscouncil.ky.gov.

To begin, I will share my story based on this template:

> I am from books and from *Amazing Grace* and Burley tobacco.
> I am from hand-sewn quilts and impeccably dressed women.
> I am from the Route 1 farm in Allensville and the Poplar Street
>   homestead in Elkton.
> I am from the front yard peonies, backyard garden and stable
>   and the tobacco fields and chicken coops.
> I am from grace and hard work.
> I am from Pat and Mayme, and Wilma and Annie, the
>   Dickersons and the Bells.
> I am from the "all talk at the same time" and the
>   contemplative.
> From "go outside and play" and the "be still and listen."
> I'm from Phillips Chapel CME and the children's choir and
>   "this little light of mine."
> I'm from damson plum preserves, chess pie, green tomato cat-
>   sup, homemade ice cream and freshly brewed iced tea with
>   every dinner.

I'm from Todd County, Kentucky.

I'm from George Dickerson who changed his name after
   freedom, and

I'm from Jeremiah McClain's Trail of Tears stop.

Now, here is the blank template with prompters for you to complete:

THE "WHERE I'M FROM" TEMPLATE

I am from _____, [*specific ordinary item*]

from _____, [*product name*]

and _____. [*produce name*]

I am from the _____ [*home description*]

_____. [*adjective, adjective sensory detail*]

I am from the _____, [*plant, flower, or natural item*]

the _____. [*plant, flower, or natural item detail*]

I am from _____, [*family tradition*]

and _____, [*family trait*]

from _____, [*name of family member*]

and _____, [*another family name*]

and _____. [*family name*]

I am from the _____, [*description of family tendency*]

and _____, [*another one*]

From _____, [*something you were told as a child*]

and _____, [*another*]

I am from _____, [*representation of religion or lack of it*]

_____. [*further description*]

I'm from _____, [*place of birth and family ancestry*]

_____. [*two food items representing your family*]

From the _____ [*specific family story about a specific
person and detail*]

the _____. [*another detail about another family member*]

CHAPTER 5

Learn from Others

"But when women are moved and lend

help, when women, who are by nature

calm and controlled, give encouragement

and applause, when virtuous and

knowledgeable women grace the endeavor

with their sweet love, then it is invincible."

—*José Martí*

I have been blessed with opportunities beyond belief to hear from, meet, and develop relationships and friendships with some outstanding early childhood leaders. Earlier in my career as a center director, I kept a poster of African American early childhood pioneers in my office. The poster included Jerri

Daniel, Carol Brunson Day, Maurice Sykes, Asa Hilliard, Barbara Bowman, and others. They were role models for me even though I didn't know them at that time. Sometimes as I think back to the professional relationships I've benefitted and learned from, I'm still amazed. From meeting the late Barbara Sizemore to Jerri Daniel, Carol Brunson Day, and Maurice Sykes, to Luis Hernandez, Jamilah J'ordan, Linda Hassan Anderson, Toni Walters, Holly Elissa Bruno, Valora Washington, Janice Hale, Jim Young, and Barbara Willer, these folks have impacted my early childhood education career in ways I couldn't have imagined, and in ways I'm sure they don't know they did. From me they all receive a standing ovation for the role they played in my career.

I took advantage of every opportunity that presented itself to network with and learn from them. Jessye N. Adams changed my life. She provided me with the opportunity for my first real, self-sustaining job in the early childhood field. Jessye N. Adams was a woman who believed in and demonstrated servant leadership. She gave back to the child care community, her church community, and her family. In 1990, at a time when I had quit a job because of the institutional racism I encountered, Ms. Adams called me and said, "I have a job for you." The job was a project position, a temporary job of six months with the opportunity to become permanent, within the state Department of Licensing in the Bureau of Child Care Licensing. Family child care was a relatively new licensing phenomenon, and the other licensors weren't really embracing those programs, so I was assigned the licensing and regulation of those programs. I took on that job with all of my being. I studied the rules and regulations and observed my colleagues and supervisors. When the time came to take the state exam for the position, I was number one on the list, and the permanent position was mine! I couldn't believe I was actually making a salary that allowed me to live a life where I wasn't struggling from paycheck to paycheck and could provide for my daughters a lifestyle they deserved.

Some years later, Jessye was there with me, literally, when my career took another step forward and I was in a meeting to negotiate my salary. She just sat patiently in the next room and waited until I came out, and we went to dinner to celebrate my promotion. One Saturday afternoon, out of the blue,

Jessye N. Adams called me, said she was in the neighborhood, and asked if she could come by. We spent some time together that day talking, laughing, eating lunch, and just sharing stories with each other. Several weeks later, one of our friends and colleagues, Ruby Snowden, called to tell me that Jessye had passed away. Pancreatic cancer, the news of which she had shared with only a couple of very close friends, had taken her life. As I mourned her, I realized that she had said goodbye to me on that Saturday afternoon. She knew that she was dying and chose to spend some time with me before she did, and I am forever grateful for her, both for who she was as a person and for the powerful impact she had on my life.

One of my most memorable opportunities was meeting Dr. Asa Hilliard, who was a noted educator, psychologist, and historian and the Fuller E. Callaway Professor of Urban Education at Georgia State University. I was working as a Wisconsin child care licensing specialist, and my supervisor, Jessye N. Adams, approved my request to attend a professional development opportunity. It was around the spring of 1992, and Wisconsin was hosting the Midwest NAEYC Conference, when they still had regional conferences. Asa Hilliard was one of the keynote plenary speakers, and I wanted to hear him speak. I had read some of his works, including *What Is Quality Child Care* by Asa Hilliard and Bettye M. Caldwell, and I really wanted to take advantage of this opportunity to hear him in person. Sitting in the former Milwaukee Auditorium, I listened and clung to every word he said; I may still have my notes from that day! I had never experienced anyone speak so intellectually, passionately, and succinctly, affirming my beliefs about teaching Black children and providing the kind of early childhood environment and curriculum they needed in order for them to be successful. "Baba," as he was known to the African American community, spoke to my soul that day, and I felt like I was the only one in the auditorium.

I returned to the office that afternoon, empowered and reenergized about my work on behalf of young children, and shared my experience with Jessye. To this day, I don't know what strings she pulled or who she called; all I know is that we were guests that evening at a private dinner with Dr. Hilliard and some of the Wisconsin early childhood leaders, and I had another opportunity to hear this man speak to my soul.

The next day at work, Jessye gave me a copy of *Testing African American Students*, a reissued book in which Dr. Hilliard was the guest editor and which he had personally signed for her. It is still one of my treasured possessions, not just because Dr. Hilliard signed it, but because Jessye thought enough of me and my interest in the subject that she wanted to make it a gift for me. That's what great leaders and mentors do: they provide opportunities for the next generation of leaders to grow. She set the example and the bar for my interactions with the women that I have had the privilege to mentor.

One of my young mentees, Ashley Lee, wrote to me in a card, "I don't know what I have done to earn your love, trust, and friendship, but I am thankful for it." One day Ashley and I were at a picnic that was hosted by a colleague of ours when Ruby Snowden, one of my mentors, arrived. I had the privilege of meeting Ruby while working with Jessye N. Adams, and she too became a mentor for me. While Jessye provided me with professional advice, Ruby offered advice on personal growth and development. That day at the picnic as we sat and chatted, I introduced Ruby to Ashley and shared with Ruby that Ashley was surprised and didn't quite understand why I was mentoring her. Ruby politely shared with Ashley that it is because that's what is expected of me—that in the same way I was mentored by Ruby and others, they expected me to do the same for others. Ashley responded that she got it "loud and clear." I think she now understands that I've had the awesome present of being mentored by some wonderful folks, and it's my obligation and duty to pay that forward. My blessing is now my mentees' blessing.

Role Models and Mentors

There have been other phenomenal women in my life as role models and mentors. Some I learned from in person, while others I observed from a distance in order to learn from them. I firmly believe that "to whom much is given, much is expected." I've been so fortunate in my life to have experienced and been lifted up by women mentors. These women took time out of their busy lives to guide, listen to, advise, and counsel me at some point in my life or during my career, and they each came into my life during a time of change or challenge. I have been graced by many women who took me under their wings and mentored me, and, as Ruby confirmed, I am obligated to do the same.

The field of early childhood education is, for the most part, a female-dominated profession. As such, we have a unique opportunity and, I would say, obligation, to support, nurture, encourage, and mentor the next generation of female leaders in our field, just as the women highlighted here have done for me. I'm not advocating by any means that early childhood education should be thought of as a "women's" or "feminist" issue. However, it must be considered and on the table when discussing issues related to job/workforce equality and equity. Available, affordable child care has enabled women (and men) to enter into and stay in the workforce, but at the same time, the child care workforce (mostly women) is often paid at little more than poverty wages, and some qualify to supplement their low wages with food stamps and Medicaid. Many members of that workforce are disproportionately women of color. As the current national dialogue and movement continues to professionalize the early childhood education field, there are many who are raising issues related to the potential impact this will have on those women of color and their pathway in this new professionalization movement. Many are concerned that these women will be left out or driven out of the workforce if professionalization happens—that they will not have the resources or support to acquire the education that will be required of this new early childhood profession.

This is not the first time this type of concern has surfaced and been discussed. As a young woman, I remember the debates that occurred around the Black woman's role in the feminist movement. I recall being present when the Black women who were my elders discussed the pros and cons of the movement, sometimes quite heatedly. Some of them believed that the feminist movement wasn't inclusive of them. From their perspective, the feminist movement was thought of as being for middle-class white women who wanted more reproductive rights and freedom to work outside the home. I vividly recall one of them saying, "We [Black women] have always worked!" They saw the feminist movement as not being inclusive of their concerns about racial inequality and the injustice that they and their families were experiencing in addition to the social and political inequity the feminist movement was addressing. So African American women coined another phrase to describe their activism. They called themselves "womanists" to better describe the holistic concerns of the intersectionality of racism, poverty, gender, and class of their agenda. "Womanism" had a more inclusive focus on the family and the wholeness of the entire Black community and justice against racial oppression of women and men. The author Alice Walker said of womanism, "Womanist is to feminist as purple to lavender" (1983, xii). So as the early childhood profession continues to evolve and as we continue to advocate for the important work we do, for the potential impact that quality early childhood education can have on our society, and for the people doing the work, I hope that we learn lessons from the past. I hope we truly consider who's at the table for the discussions and decision making and that our vision is inclusive of all the people doing the work.

> *"We are here to speak your names because*
> *of the way you made for us. Because of the*
> *prayers you prayed for us. We are the ones*
> *you conjured up, hoping we would have*
> *strength enough, and discipline enough,*
> *and talent enough, and nerve enough to*
> *step into the light when it turned in our*
> *direction, and just smile awhile."*
>
> *—Pearl Cleage,* We Speak Your Names

JACKIE ROSS

Jackie Ross was the co-owner and executive director of Utopia Child Care Center, and she gave me my first job in early childhood education. She demonstrated an incredible ability to balance high expectations and a no-nonsense approach while supporting staff professional development. Jackie Ross allowed for my managerial growth. It was as her employee that I was able to participate in the inaugural infant/toddler training in Milwaukee and thereby become one of the first people in Wisconsin to be approved to care for children under two years of age in an out-of-home setting. She also provided opportunities for me to participate in child care teacher and center director trainings put on by various organizations and an apprenticeship program at the local technical college, as well as the opportunity to receive my first credit for college course work. She was the first person not related to me that assisted with my professional development along the early childhood career pathway. Jackie Ross believed in and trusted me and my abilities, but it was only after I had demonstrated my competence to be a good teacher and staff member. Don't get me wrong, we didn't always agree, and I sometimes became frustrated with her when she held me to such high standards, but I now appreciate so much the standard she set and the role model she was for me. Mrs. Ross modeled for me how to acknowledge and grow the qualities of individual staff members. She had a center of very diverse staff members, yet based on what I observed, each one felt recognized for their strengths and empowered as individuals.

JANET HICKLIN

Janet Hicklin was the instructional leader of the early childhood associate degree program at MATC during the period that I attended. Janet too believed in my ability, probably more than I did at the time, and shared that belief with me and others. I had become a single parent and realized that I needed to further my education in order to provide a better living for myself and my young daughters, so I returned to school and was one of the older students in my cohort. Janet provided an incredible amount of positive guidance and support during my two years in the associate degree program; however, it was only after I established myself as a credible student. I remember sharing with Janet the story of my mother and grandmother and their roles in education and saying to her, "Some believe that education is in my blood and comes naturally to me." Janet replied enthusiastically and said, to my surprise, "And they are right!"

In addition to Janet, there were others at MATC who played a significant role in my professional development and career advancement, including instructor Jessie Zola and associate dean Phyllis Jelich. During my second year of the MATC associate degree program, I was asked to serve as the student representative to the MATC early childhood advisory committee. After serving that term, I was approached by Phyllis Jelich, who asked me to become a standing member of the committee and to serve as chair. I hesitated in taking on this role; however, Phyllis assured me that she and the staff believed I could do it and that she would support me in the role. As I chaired my first advisory meeting, Dean Jelich sat beside me and coached me through the agenda.

Today I often receive compliments on how efficiently I run a meeting, and I realize that it goes back to that day when Phyllis sat beside me and provided me with the invaluable lessons of how to chair a meeting. Who's providing you with lessons now that you will be able to leverage in the future?

PAT FRANKE

Pat Franke was my "twofer"! When I was hired as a child care licensing specialist, my office was right behind Pat Franke's. Pat was well known around Milwaukee and Wisconsin as the child care regulation and licensing guru. She wrote the Wisconsin child care licensing rules and regulations and led the trainings for the licensors. The offices in the state office building for those of our classification were not private. They were an early version of cubicles, so I had the good fortune to overhear some of Pat's conversations and how she interacted with licensees, concerned citizens, and bureaucrats alike. I say "some" because I also had the good sense and "home training" to not listen when not appropriate. Over the course of my four-year tenure as a child care licensor, Pat taught me that a woman making a presentation to a group with a male majority should wear red. She said it says "power" and attracts and keeps their focus. She also taught me to size up or read a room when you first enter it. She said it is important to note who's talking to whom and who's leading conversations. She said it is beneficial to try to determine who the leader is in the room.

Pat also taught me how to write an objective narrative, a skill I use to this day—possibly to the chagrin of others. Years later in a letter of recommendation Pat wrote, she penned a glowing endorsement for me that included characteristics like *self-starter, intelligent, untouchable work ethic*, and *impeccably dressed*.

EVELYN K. MOORE

I came to know some of my most influential mentors during my early years as a member of the National Black Child Development Institute (NBCDI). The cofounder and leader of NBCDI, Evelyn K. Moore, and some of the Elders of NBCDI would become mentors and advisors to me, some up close and personal and others from afar. Evelyn was a teacher in the renowned Perry Preschool Project prior to the founding of NBCDI in 1970. She founded an organization where those of us who are African American and early childhood leaders could find a home. Evelyn became a proponent of my leadership later in my career and counseled me on how to leave my legacy in the field. She founded an organization where our Elders, the keepers of our heritage, also prepared for our future. During NBCDI conferences, we could meet and network with those we had read, admired, and revered. Nurturing new emerging early childhood leaders was modeled for me by the NBCDI Elders. These African American early childhood pioneers affirmed and supported me and my role in education.

Evelyn founded an organization where there was a personal connection between members and the NBCDI staff; a sense of community was established—a network of professionals and friends, and Evelyn was like a mother to us all, leading the way. She modeled commitment for us, and we followed her example. She was surprised (though she shouldn't have been) when thousands of us showed up for the annual conference that took place right after 9/11 in 2001. As we arrived at the hotel, she was there and greeted us with hugs.

ANITA DEFRANTZ

Anita DeFrantz, a NBCDI Elder at the time I met her, now an Ancestor, wrote in 1975 what I consider one of the most comprehensive papers on Africanized English, or what was typically called *Black English* or *Ebonics*. She was also a "quiet woman" who carried herself with pride and dignity. I met Dr. DeFrantz when I was in New Orleans attending an NBCDI national conference. I was traveling alone and had arrived at the conference early enough to take in some of the city's culture. I went to Café du Monde, received my order of beignets and coffee, and looked around for somewhere to seat myself. I decided to join two women, who looked somewhat familiar and friendly, sitting together and enjoying their own morning meal. I introduced myself and so did they. One woman was Cleo Banks, one of the first (if not the first) African American teachers at the Little Red Schoolhouse. The other woman introduced herself as Anita DeFrantz. I was stunned and asked, "Are you *the* Anita DeFrantz?" to which she replied with a witty smile, "Well, I'm one of them," referencing, of course, her daughter, who is also named Anita DeFrantz and who was at the time probably more popular than her mother as the first African American woman to serve on the International Olympic Committee. It was around that time that the younger Anita DeFrantz had been elected vice president of that organization, thus inspiring her mother's comment and acknowledgement of her daughter's achievement. Anita DeFrantz asked me that day about my career, what I hoped to accomplish, and what impact I wanted to have on the field. Talk about intimidating! However, I shared with her my aspirations of making a difference in my community on the quality of early childhood education for African American children, and she advised me on which sessions I should attend at the conference.

Whenever we were at conferences together after that, we found time to sit and chat and catch up as she wrapped herself in one of the scarves she was known to wear. When Anita passed away in 2008, I attended her funeral to pay my respects. One of her sons attended the next NBCDI annual conference and brought with him several of Anita's scarves. I was fortunate enough to be the first to select a scarf. I still wrap myself in that scarf at times when I need to ponder a decision or take a stand. I like to think that she's still pushing me to think about the potential impact I can have on the lives of our children.

BURNECE BRUNSON

During another of my early NBCDI conferences, I was by myself looking for a place to have my lunch, when I was invited to sit down and was befriended by "Mother" Burnece Brunson. We had a wonderful conversation about the organization and the conference and what I could expect. She shared with me on that day some sage advice I remember to this day. One of the things she shared with me as we talked was that "NAEYC is good for your head, but NBCDI is good for your head and your heart." During subsequent NBCDI conferences, she and I would always find a way to spend time together and catch up. She allowed me time to let her know what was going on in my career and life. Mother Brunson was a published author. I have five of her books. She would often give me bits of advice when signing these books for me. In 2001 she penned, "Ann, Life can be hard sometimes—face it—and celebrate the opportunity to overcome it. Continue to be a mentor and a mentee and we will continue to have something to celebrate!" How great is that and how fortunate am I to have had someone like her in my corner? Her books have a place in my library alongside the other writers I admire: Toni Morrison, Ntozake Shange, Maya Angelou, Nikki Giovonni, Pearl Cleage, and Alice Walker—she's right there next to Hillary Clinton and Marian Wright Edelman. I was last able to spend time with Mother Brunson in 2015 when she attended the opening keynote plenary of the NAEYC annual conference. Mother Brunson passed away in January 2018 at 102 years of age. Befittingly,

I attended her memorial service with one of my mentees, Tamara Johnson. Mother Brunson would've approved.

BARBARA BOWMAN

I was introduced to Barbara Bowman via a presentation she made at one of the annual NBCDI conferences. I was first struck by how much she looked like my grandmother and, once I got past that, was awed by the highly intellectual, quiet but firm manner in which she presented the information. She spoke with authority and didn't hesitate to professionally disagree and stand firm on whatever position she was taking.

Early on in the formation of the Milwaukee County Early Childhood Council, I invited Dr. Bowman and Jamilah J'ordan to come to Milwaukee and address the council in regard to some of the work and research that had been accomplished in the Chicago Early Childhood Centers program and the family child care centers quality improvement projects. The day after they presented, one of my white colleagues called and exclaimed through the phone that Barbara Bowman was Black! I responded by saying that yes, I was aware of that fact. She then proceeded to go on and on about her ethnicity, which I found to be rather comical and that revealed to me, and I hope to her, the complexity of the perception of race. Barbara and I became better acquainted after that, and even more so after I was elected to the NAEYC Governing Board, of which she was a past president. When Barack Obama became president of the United States and his early childhood agenda was rolled out, I remember thinking how on point it was. Later I would come to understand perhaps some of the reasons why, as Barbara's daughter, Valerie Jarrett, was named Obama's senior advisor.

Graceful Inspirations

Sometimes inspiration can come not up close and personal but from people who inspire you, whose words and passion resonate with your very being. Here's a list of people who have inspired me on my leadership journey.

CORA L. MAYO

Dr. Cora L. Mayo, PhD, was a leader at Black Experience Inc., a publisher of early childhood educational materials. She and I also met at an NBCDI conference. We happened to sit together at one of the sessions and struck up a conversation. To my surprise and delight, shortly after returning home from the conference, I received a package in the mail from Cora that included several of her publications on educating Black children and a couple of children's books. Cora passed on May 19, 2014. Her funeral was held at the DuSable Museum of African American History in Chicago, Illinois. In reading her obituary, I was not surprised to learn that she was one of a group of Black educators who came together in 1972 at the inaugural Operation PUSH (People United Save Humanity) Expo to plan and present an alternative plan to the educational system at the time.

ADELAIDE SANFORD

Adelaide Sanford . . . my, oh my. Dr. Adelaide Sanford, "Queen Mother" Sanford, is an educator and activist and Vice Chancellor Emeritus Board of Regents of the State University of New York. She is an elder in the African tradition and one of the most sincere advocates for Black children and their education that I have met. When she speaks, she opens the address with the words, "My beloved ones." Her very presence exudes greatness and tells you that you're in the presence of someone special, while at that same time she is unpretentious and unassuming about her own special presence. Dr. Sanford calls the achievement gap an *access, opportunity, resource,* and *expectation gap,* removing the responsibility from the children and placing it on the adults responsible for the resources. She explains how we can address some of the chaos and dysfunction in the African American community with a simple story. The story is about a woman who's lost a precious jewel, and she's looking around, searching fervently for her lost jewel. Soon a crowd of people gather and attempt to help her find her jewel. They are all searching, turning over every rock and peering into every corner, looking for this jewel. Then along comes a man who inquires about the search, and the woman explains that they are looking for her lost jewel. Then the man asks the most important question of all: "Is this where you lost the jewel?" And the woman answers, "No, this is where the light is." Dr. Sanford explains that the Black community cannot focus on where others tell us we've "lost" our children, where others are shining the light. Dr. Sanford instead seems to suggest that the Black community should identify the challenges and the solutions for assisting our children to realize their full potential. I invited Dr. Sanford to be the keynote speaker at the Embracing Diversity Conference in Milwaukee so that others could hear her powerful messages.

Graceful Colleagues

During my career, I've also had the privilege and honor of knowing some dynamic early childhood leaders. These women have also impacted my professional career.

VANESSA RICH

In 2002 I served as an adjunct faculty member of MATC in the early childhood education associate degree program. As such, one of the faculty invited me to participate in the Wheelock College Early Childhood Higher Education Faculty Initiative. The goal of this initiative was to provide the opportunity for teams to learn from one another and to better plan to meet the professional development needs of the Head Start staff members in their area. It was at this event that I met Vanessa Rich. If I recall correctly, at that time Vanessa was working for the Chicago Head Start program and was one of the presenters for that professional learning opportunity. Vanessa came in like a whirlwind and unashamedly spoke on behalf of those not at the table, the Black and brown children and their families that the Head Start programs were serving. When she received questions and sometimes pushback from the (usually white) participants, she stood firm in the information she presented and in the "why" of her message. I remember thinking to myself, who is this woman who stands so firm in what she believes? Is this the education and care we should be providing to our kids? How is she so comfortable in speaking so openly on matters that we, Black people, usually talk about with one another?

Later in the day when Vanessa and I had the opportunity to sit and talk, she plainly and very directly told me that our children didn't have time for us to be polite about their educational needs and that she had had too many experiences of "others" trying to tell her what our kids needed. Vanessa Rich left an impression on me that day and modeled how to stand firm in speaking truth to power. I had yet not had the experience of white colleagues challenging me, my expertise, my authority, or my intelligence. However, when those times came, and there have been plenty, I remembered Vanessa and stood firm in my truth. Vanessa and I didn't see each other often, but when we did, it was like no time had passed since the first and last time we'd met. The early childhood community lost a staunch advocate when Vanessa Rich passed away in December 2015. The Head Start community, which she loved, remembered her as "a brilliant and formidable leader, and a kind, devoted friend" (National Head Start Association, accessed 2018). That was Vanessa Rich.

JANICE HALE

Dr. Janice Hale was a beacon of light for the education of African American children until her death in 2017. She was steadfast in her mission to provide information and education to people working with or on behalf of African American children. She did this via her books: *Black Children: Their Roots, Culture, and Learning Styles* (1982); *Unbank the Fire: Visions for the Education of African American Children* (1994); and *Learning While Black: Creating Educational Excellence for African American Children* (2001). The latter two were both nominated for a Pulitzer Prize. She also advocated for and helped others advocate for Black children when she founded the Institute for the Study of the African American Child (ISAAC). In 2007 when I first heard from Janice about ISAAC, I was struck by her unrelenting determination to create the change she believed was needed for African American children to succeed in school. ISAAC was to be the vehicle and infrastructure for that change, which included creating a community of scholars, school district leaders, researchers, educators, civil rights leaders, politicians, and the African American general public. She believed that if we built the infrastructure, then we would be in a position to influence public policy that affects African American children. And for those of us who became fellows and members of ISAAC and attended the conferences, she made believers out of us as well.

GWEN T. JACKSON

From 2000 to 2008, I had the privilege of being appointed to the Milwaukee County Early Childhood Council, and I served as the chair from 2004 to 2006. The woman who preceded me as chair of the council was Gwen T. Jackson, another staunch early childhood advocate. While Gwen's career wasn't early childhood focused, she nonetheless understood the importance of high-quality early childhood education, especially for the most vulnerable children. Gwen's involvement in advancing the lives of Milwaukee's children began in the late 1950s, when she was on the Family Life Committee of the Milwaukee Urban League. A predominate issue even at that time was providing quality child care throughout Milwaukee. And so the advocacy journey of Gwen Jackson began. In 1961 Gwen began what would be a career calling: her Red Cross career. She started as a volunteer and rose to one of the highest volunteer positions in the organization, National Chair of Volunteers, from 1988 through 1992. Gwen and I became friends, and she modeled for me, even in her senior years, how an individual voice can make a difference in the lives of children. In 2009 the Division of Early Childhood Education put forth a recommendation and the Milwaukee Board of School Directors voted to approve the renaming of the former Twenty-first Street School after Mrs. Jackson— another testament to her work on behalf of children. I saw Gwen recently at a community event, and even though she's now in a wheelchair and her sight is fading, she's making decisions about what issues are important and deserve her support and her voice.

These women all played such a significant role in the development of my professional career. They have each contributed in their own way to the field of early childhood education while some were also being leaders in the African American community. They led with integrity and authenticity and modeled humility and empathy, and they were inspirational! In his *Inc.com* article, Jeff Haden lists the following "8 Ways to Be a Truly Memorable Boss"; I believe these qualities can also be attributed to great mentors: "They believe the unbelievable; they see opportunity in instability and uncertainty; they wear their emotions on their sleeves; they protect others from the bus; they've been there, done that, and still do that; they lead by permission, not authority; they embrace a larger purpose; and they take real risks, not fake risks" (2013). I have been so fortunate in my life and career to have such women guide and nurture me, and I believe that it is my responsibility to be that for the next generation of leaders.

In her 2009 *Exchange Magazine* article "Lifting as You Climb," Debra Ren-Etta Sullivan writes, "We often talk about 'growing our own leaders,' but this seems to be more difficult than it sounds. Growing our own leaders means that current leaders need to mentor the next generation of leaders." She goes on to address what she calls "scarcity thinking"; that is, that those of us in leadership positions are hesitant to mentor because we feel a need to retain those roles for ourselves. Instead of scarcity thinking, Debra promotes "abundance thinking." She says, "Children require an abundance of leadership."

> *"Behind every successful woman is a tribe of other successful women who have her back."*
>
> —*author unknown*

Find Your Mentors

As I have previously stated, I've been very fortunate to have some remark-able women as mentors and role models for me, both professionally and per-sonally. How can you build your own network of role models and mentors? Take a look at who you currently have in your circle and then make note of who else you'd like to have the opportunity to meet and have conversations with. You may want to consider these steps:

- Be bold in introducing yourself to someone you admire and want to know better. Recently a young woman and I had an email exchange that was work related. At the end of the work "conversation," she asked if I'd like to have coffee sometime. I said yes, and we met and had a wonder-ful conversation. Toward the end of the meeting, she asked if I'd be will-ing to continue to meet with and mentor her. I was quite flattered by this because I consider her to be a wonderfully intelligent up-and-coming young woman. I said yes, I'd be happy to continue to meet and continue our great dialogues.

- Get to know the names and faces of leaders you admire. You never know when the opportunity will present itself for you to meet—have your elevator speech ready!

- Present yourself professionally and be prepared every day for that opportunity when it comes. There can't be much worse than having an opportunity come your way and not being prepared to take it on.

- Don't let distance keep you from being mentored by someone you admire. I shared earlier in this chapter that I once kept a poster of Afri-can American early childhood pioneers in my office. I looked up to these folks from afar. I read their works and enthusiastically embraced their ideas, ideals, and philosophies. Since that time, I've found out that others have been watching me from afar as I did some of my role models. I was recently surprised when serving on a local committee to be introduced by Lamonte Blades, someone I considered a colleague, as her mentor. Later on she told me that she has always admired me and considered me a mentor.

CHAPTER 6

Create Leaders

A great leader produces other leaders. Real leaders leave behind some real way for those that come behind them to carry on—or, said a little more bluntly, if you're leading and nobody's following, you're just out for a walk! Those in leadership positions must lead, follow, or get out of the way.

Succession Planning

During the launch of his foundation's first program initiative in 2017, President Barack Obama said that one of the best ways for him to have an impact on the future is by training the next generation of leaders. One of the best lessons in succession planning that I've observed was through the organization Milwaukee Film. Milwaukee Film is responsible for the yearly planning and implementation of the two-week-long Milwaukee Film Festival. The mission of Milwaukee Film is to "entertain, educate, and engage" the Milwaukee community through cinematic experience. One day during the festival, I had a chance to observe the line of folks waiting to get into the theater for the next film showing. I noticed that most of the people in line appeared to be at least sixty years of age or older. These folks didn't look any different than those I've seen in other Milwaukee Film Festival lines. However, I also know that Milwaukee Film has recognized that in order to increase and maintain its membership and keep the organization viable, it must increase the number of young, diverse members. And so the organization put in place a very intentional plan to do just that.

Milwaukee Film began to show more films by young, diverse producers and directors, and it started a program at several of the local high schools. This was done via the successful Black Lens and Cine Sin Fronteras programming. My colleague and friend Mark Sabljak, Milwaukee Film Corporate and Community Engagement director, credits the executive director, Jonathan Jackson, with the majority of the leadership in also taking on education-related programming to increase the diversity of the membership and participants. They've added programming that sends filmmakers into local schools to discuss their careers with students, student screenings during the festival, and teacher fellowships. Many of us can learn from Milwaukee Film and the intentional way it is keeping the organization viable well into the future.

Think about your own group or organization. Whose voice and presence is missing from the table? How do you invite people in and allow them to feel comfortable and part of the organization? How are you planning to sustain your organization and position it for future growth and viability? I once heard a parable about the aspen tree. While on the surface a grove of aspen trees may look like all individual trees, underneath they are interconnected with a common root system. I like to think of the teams that I've been fortunate enough to lead in that way. Although we are all individuals, when we form a team, there is an interconnectedness that brings us together as a community of leaders working on behalf of children and families.

For five years, I was the cochair of a team that led an effort to bring a national-type conference to Milwaukee, the Embracing Diversity Conference. We were able to underwrite the cost of the conference by allocating some of the funding reserved for professional development in the grant budget that I had oversight of. The vision was to bring to the Milwaukee early childhood community a conference that equaled in every respect a national-level conference, and we successfully accomplished that from 2002 to 2007. Each year we invited national keynote speakers and presenters, many of whom are the people I've spoken of here, as well as others, including Asa Hilliard, Adelaide Sanford, Carol Brunson Day, Burnece Brunson, Holly Elissa Bruno, Luis Hernandez, Maurice Sykes, Toni Walters, Debra Ren-Etta Sullivan, Cecelia Alvarado, Pam Winton, Melinda Green, Crystal Kuykendall, Leonard Pitts, Evelyn K. Moore, Aisha Ray, Jawanza Kunjufu, and Janet Gonzalez-Mena, just to name a few.

My vision for this conference was to provide a high-level professional development opportunity to the Milwaukee early childhood education community, many of whom were Black and brown child care providers who did not have the funds to participate in a national conference, and to present to them national early childhood leaders who were also people of color, allowing them to be introduced to the people who were influencing me and the early childhood profession. This conference became so successful that we were asked to open it up for participation statewide and received inquiries from around the country from those interested in replicating the conference. As a result of the conference, I was nominated for a Bammy Award in 2005 by Holly Elissa Bruno, who believed that the conference should become a national one.

In 2005 we also identified and celebrated about a dozen emerging leaders in the Milwaukee early childhood community. Delechia Johnson was one of those emerging leaders recognized. She was then, and still is, one of the best early childhood trainers I've ever met. She has a way of connecting with the students, incorporating that method of "firm, fair, friendly," and clueing in to the individual student's needs. I've often gone to her for advice for teaching certain classes. She says of being recognized that year, "It was a turning point in my career because I didn't see myself as a leader. . . . That day I had to realize my destiny as a leader. There was no intentionality to create the next leaders until the Embracing Diversity Conference. We got to see people of color who were doing great things nationally." When Delechia graduated from Erikson Institute, she wrote me the nicest letter that was tucked inside her graduation invitation. In it she thanked me for being a role model and mentor. She stated that while it wasn't formal mentoring, she had been observing and learning from me. We now have a more formal mentoring relationship.

Becoming a Mentor

Leading the Embracing Diversity Conference allowed me to have some influence on the larger Milwaukee early childhood community. However, while on my own leadership journey, it's been my pleasure to mentor a number of women in the education field. After all, to be a leader, you must also be a bridge, creating new pathways across obstacles for others. In these mentoring relationships, I've learned as much from these women as they've learned from me.

Some leaders come by their leadership ability naturally and improve and build upon the set of skills they have. However, others of us must learn how to lead. Developing the capacity to lead and the ability to develop leadership skills aren't accomplished overnight. Successful leadership requires vision, people skills, emotional intelligence, and self-discipline on the part of the person wanting to lead. Like any other skill set, it requires study, practice, and time.

It's always been my goal to lead my team and treat them in a way that I would like to be treated. I learn and work best in an environment where I have time to think about my input into a decision or meeting, so I'd like to know up front what the meeting topic will be so that I can prepare. If that is not possible, I need enough time to think about my input, and I need for the leader to really listen to what I have to say. I'm always conscious that people have different ways of being part of and participating in group situations. A mentoring relationship incorporates some of these same components. As a trusted guide, a mentor has the ability to assist the mentee in achieving professional goals and success.

"The signs of outstanding leadership

appear primarily among the followers.

Are the followers reaching their potential?

Are they learning? Serving? Do they

achieve the required results? Do they

change with grace? Manage conflict?"

—*Max Depree,* Leadership Is an Art

"I learned from the BEST!! Thank you for being part of and guiding my journey." This note was sent to me by Tamara Johnson in response to my congratulating her on an accomplishment and finding her voice. Tamara is the mentee who is probably the closest to me who never worked directly for me. I noticed her when she was a student in one of the evening classes I taught at MATC. She was a standout student and had a lot of untapped potential. She wasn't shy to talk about her struggles and challenges, and I personally wanted to make sure that she had every opportunity for her professional growth and development. She took advantage of every opportunity I presented to her, and then she started identifying opportunities for herself and became her own advocate. After receiving her associate degree in 2003, she has gone on to attain her bachelor's degree (2006) and master's degree (2016). For five years, she has been the executive director of Malaika Early Learning Center where, under her leadership, the center has become a five-star-rated center under the Wisconsin YoungStar quality rating system and is also nationally accredited by NAEYC. Last year the center expanded and added a charter school, now serving children through age eight. Tamara was elected to the NAEYC Governing Board in March 2017 to serve a four-year term.

Sonja Smith-Pica and Candace Armstrong are two mentees that demonstrated to me personal strength and fortitude like none I'd seen before. I learned so much about pride and perseverance from these two young women. Around 2000, when I was the director of WECA, we received a grant from the Milwaukee Early Childhood Council for the provision of technical assistance and quality improvement grants for Milwaukee-based child care centers. An important component of this project was that in order to participate, the centers had to have their programs evaluated using the ITERS, ECERS, and SACERS early childhood environmental rating scales. One of my goals at the time was to bring more qualified people of color into leadership opportunities, so I selected Sonja and Candace to be among those who would be trained in the implementation of the environmental rating scales. I knew these two young women from my MATC classes and knew that they were intelligent and could handle the job. They, along with several others, went through training with Thelma Harms, the developer of the environmental rating scales, and her team. They rated so highly in their reliability training that Thelma said that she'd hire them as assessors for her program if they lived in North Carolina, and she called them the "anchors" in Wisconsin for the environmental scales.

Even with this kind of backing and confirmation, they were treated so badly when they went into the centers and programs that had applied to be part of the project. These programs were being administered by folks who had long seen themselves as early childhood leaders in the Milwaukee child care community, and they frankly resented these two young women of color coming into their programs to rate them. They were confronted and called "gals," and their ratings were challenged.

Around the same time, there was another initiative that was rating some of the same programs using the environmental rating scales, but the assessors were graduate students with no early childhood backgrounds and who had been trained by people who did not have environmental scales training. So the scores that Sonja and Candace presented were different than those higher scores presented by the graduate students. Even in the midst of this challenging situation, these women kept their dignity and probably only showed to me their surprise and the hurt being put upon them by these self-proclaimed leaders. I was disappointed with these people, and I let them know I believed their actions to be racist and discriminatory. I recently heard from Sonja that in March 2016 she participated in reliability training with ERSI's Cathy Riley, who had also trained her in 2000. Sonja very proudly shared with me that she "still had it," as her reliability score some sixteen years later was still 95 percent!

Kortney Smith, another mentee, is the epitome of a combination of intelligence, style, and grace. When Kortney was the Milwaukee Public Schools (MPS) Head Start director, I observed her take the lead on a particularly challenging staff situation. She methodically and patiently gathered the evidence on a staff person that had destroyed records when she didn't receive an internal promotion. I didn't have to do much in this situation. Kortney navigated through this difficult situation in a professional and transparent manner. She was firm but fair, and she set the standard and expectations for the program. When she made the decision to accept a principal position in a suburban district, I was sad to see her go, but I knew she would be a great leader for her new staff and students.

I've been fortunate to mentor and lead teams that have been made up of intelligent, focused young visionary leaders, and I've learned as much from them as they've learned from me. This new generation of leaders are strong women, standing firmly in who they are and what they bring to the table. It's exciting to watch them facilitate and contribute to the decision-making process and lead their organizations.

A Good Leader Follows

A good leader knows that sometimes you must follow, and she understands when and how to do that with grace. One of the younger leaders I've been able to "follow" is Dr. Darienne B. Driver, superintendent of MPS. Dr. Driver is an intelligent, energetic, collaborative leader who always keeps the children of MPS front and center when making decisions. She works long hours and expects those working with her to do the same. I met her when she came to MPS as the chief innovation officer. I hadn't officially been introduced to her; all I knew of her was the patter of heels going down the hallway. She didn't walk anywhere, she almost ran—as if she knew that our kids couldn't wait. So one day as I heard her coming down the hallway, I stepped out of my office and introduced myself to her. We chatted as she walked—it was hard to keep up pace with her. Some weeks later, I received notice of a meeting that I was to attend at nine o'clock that morning. At the meeting, I was offered the opportunity to work with Dr. Driver as the director of innovation projects, responsible for implementing her ideas to turn around the failing schools of the district. We worked well together and put in place programs and projects, and we did see the students of those schools improve their reading and math outcomes. When Dr. Driver became superintendent a couple of years later, she asked me to take on the leadership of the MPS Foundation and "reconstitute" it.

Dr. Driver's leadership is inspiring. In her role as superintendent, she has challenged the status quo and empowered her direct reports to put in place new and innovative programming in order to increase the academic proficiency and graduation rates of MPS students. She has created partnerships with those in the Milwaukee community that wouldn't have previously considered partnering with the district—and in fact were at odds with the school district. Dr. Driver has quickly become a respected player in the Milwaukee community and has demonstrated the following leadership qualities:

- She inspires and, in doing so, empowers her staff to deliver amazing work.

- She enables her team members to act, allowing for them to feel capable and valued.

- She models the way with energy and the creation of standards of excellence.

- She challenges the status quo and leads with her heart.

- She inspires a shared vision for the children of Milwaukee.

The ability to successfully lead a team includes a collection of skills with many facets, some of which are vision, emotional strength, people skills, respect, and discipline.

How to Create Leaders

How do leaders go about creating other leaders? What is the role of a mentor? Sometimes the role of a mentor is a more formal arrangement that is agreed upon between two individuals, and sometimes it is a less formal relationship, a happenstance. I've been involved in both types of situations. Based on my experience, here are some thoughts on how to build a successful, encouraging, and motivating mentoring relationship:

- Decide if there is really time to devote to the mentee.

- Build a trusting and respectful relationship between the mentor and mentee.

- Establish communication protocols.

- Collaboratively create a meeting schedule, especially if the mentoring is in a work environment.

- Be a good listener while maintaining confidentiality.

- Facilitate the mentee attending meetings and other events that will benefit their professional growth.

- Offer advice and guidance, but do not overprotect the mentee from experiences.

- Celebrate any successes or attained goals with the mentee.

In regard to not being overprotective and allowing mentees to make decisions and have experiences, I recently received a call from one of my mentees inquiring about a job opportunity. I immediately said to her that I didn't think she wanted the job and stated some of the reasons. After giving this some thought, I called her back and apologized for my response. I explained that I realized I was operating in a protective "mother hen" space. I reframed my response to her about the job and told her that if she decided to apply for the position, I would support her decision.

Are there opportunities for mentoring in your organization? It is important for leaders to encourage mentoring in their organizations. If done successfully, all of the parties involved benefit—the mentee, the mentor, and the organization. For the mentee, finding someone they can trust for support and guidance is beneficial; however, in many situations, the act of supporting provides the mentor with opportunities to reflect on their own circumstances, thereby also benefitting the mentor. The organization benefits by creating a pipeline of future leaders and the promotion of a more productive workplace.

CHAPTER 7

Always with Grace

"And I love that even in the toughest

moments, when we're all sweating it—

when we're worried that the bill won't

pass, and it seems like all is lost—Barack

never lets himself get distracted by

the chatter and the noise. Just like his

grandmother, he just keeps getting up and

moving forward . . . with patience and

wisdom, and courage and grace."

—Michelle Obama

Your attitude toward change or challenges can make you get up when you want to sit down or put one foot in front of the other and say, "I've got to do this." I don't believe there are mistakes in our lives—there's not one thing that has happened to me or that I have experienced that's not a valuable lesson, if I choose to see it that way. Every experience, no matter how negative, can be seen either as a stumbling block or as a stepping stone to learn more about yourself and move your life forward. I believe we have all the information we need inside of us to overcome any challenge we've had to face. We only have to "get still" and listen. I also have been able to live by the adage "Excellence is the highest form of rebellion." During one particularly challenging time for my team, as we each came out of the experience unbroken, one of the team members sent me a GIF of a striding wolf with the words, "Throw me to the wolves and I'll return leading the pack!"

> *"Being powerful is like being a lady. If you*
>
> *have to tell people you are, you aren't."*
>
> *—Margaret Thatcher*

One particular experience stands out for me, and it reminds me of the old adage, "People who shine from within don't need the spotlight." During the beginning of my term as the leader of a local organization, my ability to lead was challenged by someone who, at the time, I considered a friend and colleague. Her attack was personal and vicious, and her only reason for this behavior was so that she could take over as the leader of the organization. My integrity and leadership had never been challenged so personally before. However, unbeknownst to me, this person had a history of behaving this way to get where she wanted to go, and she had stepped on others to do so. For example, she was asked for the contact information of one of our young Milwaukee leaders by a statewide organization that wanted this emerging leader to serve on their board of directors. Instead of passing on the contact information, she said to them that the person they wanted wasn't ready and suggested that she'd be a better board member. This story was shared with me years later when the leader of the organization and I had the opportunity to be together for another meeting. Not everyone deserves a front seat in your life, and I made the decision that this person was one who didn't. I relieved myself of that burdensome relationship.

True leaders do not need to step on others to move themselves up, nor do they need to nominate themselves for awards and recognition. Author bell hooks writes, "Sometimes people try to destroy you, precisely because they recognize your power—not because they don't see it, but because they see it and they don't want it to exist" (2012, 149). If others appreciate who you are and what you do as a leader, that recognition will come naturally.

> *"One small crack does not mean you are*
>
> *broken; it means that you were put to the*
>
> *test and you didn't fall apart."*
>
> *—Linda Poindexter*

During those challenging times, my internal fortitude allowed me to not become overwhelmed with the situations and to differentiate between the experiences and my value, to be clear about who I am. People will often try to talk you out of fulfilling your purpose, but you've got to be clear about who you are. If you have to, refocus during those challenging times and remember your value and your vision.

There is a story (of course a story—remember I told you I like stories?) about two wolves. It's called "A Cherokee Tale," and it goes like this. One evening an old Cherokee told his grandson about a battle that goes on inside of people. He said, "My son, the battle is between two wolves inside us all. One is evil. It is anger, envy, jealousy, sorrow, regret, greed, arrogance, self-pity, guilt, resentment, inferiority, lies, false pride, superiority, and ego. The other is good. It is joy, peace, love, hope, serenity, humility, kindness, benevolence, empathy, generosity, truth, compassion, and faith." The grandson thought about this for a minute and then asked his grandfather, "Which wolf wins?" The old Cherokee simply replied, "The one you feed."

Grace under Pressure

I've shared with you many of the highlights of my career; however, there have been many challenging times as well. How does a graceful leader handle those moments? It takes courage to be a graceful leader in times of great challenge. Courage is the most important virtue. Without courage, you cannot practice any other virtues.

You also have to forgive yourself for any experiences you deem failures because if you had known better, you would've done better. I have found that when people don't understand my way of leading—especially people who don't have the same values or don't value what I bring to the table, people who think a lot of themselves and talk just to hear themselves talk—they assume that I'm not paying attention or have little or no input in a matter. In reality we should never assume that loud is strong and quiet is weak. We should never mistake silence for ignorance, calmness for acceptance, or kindness for weakness. A strong female leader understands that gifts such as logic, decisiveness, and strength are just as feminine as intuition and emotional connection. A strong leader values and uses all of her gifts. Sometimes being underestimated is one of the greatest competitive advantages you can have.

> *"Don't underestimate me. I know more than I say, think more than I speak, and notice more than you realize."*
>
> *—author unknown*

I once had a male supervisor who asked me to perform a work-related task that I believed was unethical—to give a relative of his a contract for some of the work I was hired to do. This was a new position in a new department for me, and this new supervisor didn't know me very well. I believe that he mistook my quiet manner for weakness. I took notes in our meeting, and when I returned to my office, I sent him an email message reminding him of and detailing for him the skill set that I brought to the position and the organization's policy on ethics and conflict of interest. He replied to my email message saying that he didn't know that I had that kind of background and, in a retaliatory manner, said from then on we would need to have face-to-face, one-on-one meetings every week. This same person also started to call me at the end of the day to ask me if I wanted to go out to have dinner. I responded politely but firmly no.

The last straw was when he was supposed to turn in a report that his supervisor had asked for. He assigned another member of his staff to produce the document but didn't submit it in time for me to include it in the package that was being produced for a meeting. He yelled at me over the phone like he was yelling at a man on the street he was getting ready to go to blows with. I immediately sent an email message to the human resources department requesting a meeting the next workday. That day I reported the whole situation to the head of human resources and was subsequently removed from his supervision.

I have several ways of dealing with challenging situations on my own terms. First, I pick my conflicts. Why try to win the battle when you can win the war? Whenever possible, I plan for those moments. I'm not good at winging it, but if I know there's a situation and I've had the opportunity to plan for it, I'm in a good place. And as I mentioned earlier in the book, a sense of calm is contagious and tells others that you're in control and can handle unexpected challenges that come your way. I also jump in when there is an opportunity and if it's a matter that I feel strongly about. Importantly, I've also been able to build a powerful network of individuals that know me, my work, and the strengths I bring to the table. When you believe in yourself, others will believe in you too. Using these techniques, I've been able to maintain my grace even when the going gets tough.

As previously stated, I've come to believe that courage is the most important virtue, because without courage you cannot practice any of the other virtues. I firmly believe that you should never compromise who you are personally to become who you want to be professionally. My moral compass made it challenging to work with the person in the above scenario. What would you do in a similar situation? Each of us has a personal perspective of right and wrong. It's those ethics, our personal code of conduct, which serve as our moral compass.

- What are your core values and beliefs?

- What is your personal code of conduct?

- Your "professional brand" is what people say about you when you're not in the room. How are you and your work being reflected upon?

- Are there changes you need to make now to ensure that your professional brand is a positive reflection of your personal mission and values?

- What will be your career legacy?

Graceful Leadership Requires Emotional Intelligence

In leading with grace, you must also possess the other leadership qualities of intelligence, toughness, determination, and vision. However, graceful leadership also requires emotional intelligence, self-awareness, self-regulation, motivation, empathy, and social skills. In closing I'd like to tie these components of leadership back to the attributes discussed in the previous chapters.

Because leadership is often seen as male-oriented, some people may not be comfortable projecting the calmness and clarity of graceful leadership. However, I'm confident that this can be overcome and people can learn this leadership style. One can have all of the cognitive abilities, technical skills, systems thinking, and strategic visioning necessary to perform a job; however, without emotional intelligence, the leader cannot be successful. What is emotional intelligence, and how do you know if someone has it?

Self-awareness is a component of emotional intelligence and includes having an understanding of your emotions: your motivations, your strengths, your challenges, your values, your goals, your job performance, the people on your team, and how all these things affect you. For example, I am not a "last-minute" type of person. If there's a deadline, my goal is to have a task completed well in advance so that I have time to review and revise if necessary. I may want a couple of other people to review my work and provide feedback. I will also submit it in advance of the due date so that if there is feedback, I have time to adjust and resubmit. The self-aware leader is reflective and can objectively self-assess. They are self-confident and understand their capabilities and will seek assistance when necessary. Authentic leaders are not afraid to show their vulnerabilities in front of others. Being tuned in to who you are as a person and being comfortable with who you are communicates a genuineness to others and will allow you to build trust with and among your team.

Self-management is another component of emotional intelligence. This is the management of your emotions and behaviors to achieve your goals. I've heard it described as having a continuous conversation with yourself. If you are able to control your feelings and impulses, you will model this for your team and establish an environment of trust among the team members. In a competitive workplace, self-control can also be an advantage. Instead of panicking when they're given a new assignment or they're facing reorganization in the workplace, the self-regulated person will seek out and take in the new information, demonstrating maturity and a "team player" mindset. These are the people supervisors rely on because their integrity, comfort with change, and thoughtfulness shine through.

Emotionally intelligent people are motivated people as well. They know what drives them to pursue their goals and ambitions. Typically these people possess a passion for their work that goes beyond financial gain or status. They have a strong drive and are high achievers. These are the leaders who challenge the status quo while also having a commitment to the organization they work for. They set the bar high for themselves, their teams, and also for their organizations.

Social awareness or empathy for others is a necessary characteristic of emotional intelligence that may seem out of place in the traditional lens of leadership. *Empathy* means thoughtfully considering and understanding others' feelings in the decision-making process. A compassionate leader is aware of and respectful of their individual team member's efforts. They should also be able to understand the team's emotional makeup and lead in a firm, fair, and friendly manner while holding everyone accountable for their work performance. The leader should be sensitive to the subtleties of body language, able to hear the messages beneath the words being spoken, and be culturally competent. If the leader is attuned to these things, she will be able to identify the needs of individual staff members and the team and identify where coaching or mentoring is appropriate. There is a skill to balancing these actions. Being compassionate and authentic with accountability can be challenging. However, the graceful leader understands that, collectively, the team members can all achieve their goals.

Social skill or one's ability to manage relationships with others is another emotional intelligence factor. Proficiently forming and managing relationships, building networks, working in teams, and dealing effectively with conflict all fall into this area. These folks have a knack for building rapport with all kinds of people, are adept at managing teams, and are excellent collaborators. These leaders build connections easily and have a wide range of acquaintances and networks. They realize that these connections may be needed one day. Remember that some relationships will come full circle.

> *"Give us grace and strength to forbear*
>
> *and to persevere. . . . Give us courage and*
>
> *gaiety and the quiet mind. Spare to us our*
>
> *friends, soften to us our enemies."*
>
> —*Robert Louis Stevenson, "We Thank*
>
> *Thee,"* Prayers Written at Vailima

Moving Forward with Grace

In June 2015, Dylann Roof, a self-professed white supremacist, walked into Emanuel African Methodist Episcopal Church in Charleston, South Carolina, and shot dead nine praying men and women. When the family of the victims came face-to-face with the shooter in the courthouse, they told him that they forgave him. There's no better example of grace. During the memorial service for Reverend Clementa Pinckney, one of the victims, President Barack Obama said, "If we can find that grace, anything is possible," and then he started to sing the hymn "Amazing Grace" (2015). The rest of the mourners soon joined in, and it became one of the defining and unifying moments that came out of that tragedy. The irony of this song and its popularity in the Black church is that it was authored by a former slave trader after his conversion to Christianity. So each time that song is sung in a Black church, there's grace—perhaps even unknown to the congregations.

I do not profess to have the grace of the victims' family members who forgave Dylann Roof. I'm not sure I know how I would react in that situation. The challenges I've experienced in my professional life do not compare with that tragedy. But in those times when my integrity, leadership ability, and expertise have been questioned and challenged, I believe that I've handled the situations with grace and dignity.

Graceful leadership allows us to remain calm when it's easier to be angry in challenging situations. Graceful leadership allows us to "be still" enough to hear what is and what isn't being said. Graceful leadership allows us to remain true to our leadership style and philosophy and not change who we are. Graceful leadership allows us to be transparent, humble enough to admit we don't know it all, and vulnerable enough to make mistakes. Graceful leadership allows us to treat people with respect.

Vision Board

I've shared previously about my use of vision boards. These are inspirational reminders of my goals and aspirations. They are my personal collages of pictures, words, or phrases meant to help me keep focused. They also give anyone who sees them a little snapshot of me and what drives me. I keep these vision boards at work and at home. The ones at work are typically focused on professional goals, and those at home are more personal. For example, the side of my refrigerator is currently serving as a vision board with lists of healthy foods, pictures of my grandkids, "drink more water" signage, and a list of foods that are part of the "best age-defying" diet. At work I've incorporated the idea of a vision board onto the office walls. There are inspirational quotes on the walls above pictures of the district students involved in the activities that we raised funds to support. Some of the quotes are "If you want to lift yourself up, lift up someone else" from Booker T. Washington's *Up from Slavery*, and "Education is for improving the lives of others and for leaving your community and world better than you found it" from Marian Wright Edelman's *The Measure of Our Success*.

You can create your own vision board. Have you ever created a collage art project with a variety of materials, typically magazines, paper, and glue? This is the same process for creating your own vision board. Gather a variety of magazines to use (you don't want all gardening magazines, for example). You will have better outcomes if you have an assortment of materials.

Once collected, page through the magazines for phrases and photos that have meaning for you. These words or pictures can represent goals, vision, memories, family, or work. I don't recommend using actual photographs; however, copies of photos that have meaning are a good substitute. Once you've gathered your materials, simply glue them to the paper in a way that means something to you. To start there may be a particular photo or phrase that resonates with you. Use that as the center of your vision board, and then move from there in whatever way strikes your fancy. Another less permanent way to create a vision board is to use the always reliable bulletin board, making it easy to edit whenever necessary. Lately I've also seen people using "word cloud" tools, which can be useful in creating your vision board.

Here's an example of my vision board:

Live with Integrity
& Lead by example

CREATE STANDARD
OF EXCELLENCE FO
OTHERS TO FOLLOW.

amazing
gRACE

≥ INSPIRE ≤
others to be
all they can be
build a great
team.

Establish
AND maintain
balance
IN YOUR LIFE.

Lead in suc
a way tha
if someone
speaks bad
about you
no one wil
believe th

"YOU'VE ALWA

my

YOU JUST

FOR

-GLINDA

CELEBRATE ACCOMPLISHMENTS

Enjoy the Journey.

Make a plan of ACTION for PERSONAL EMPOWERMENT.

RROUND YOURSELF
TH THOSE WHO SEE YOUR

greatness

ND ENCOURAGE YOU.

BE CAREFUL WHO YOU LOOK UP TO:
YOU WILL MOVE IN THE DIRECTION OF
THE PEOPLE YOU ASSOCIATE WITH.

THE POWER

ar

) LEARN IT

ELF."

) WITCH

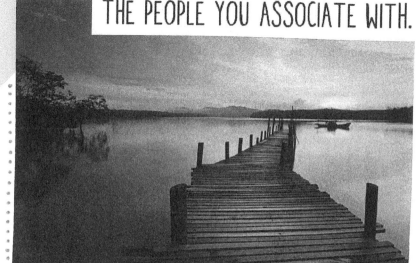

KEEP YOUR EYES ON THE PRIZE AND YOUR HANDS ON THE PLOW

References

Amirault, Chris. 2017. "Introduce Yourself." Hello forum by NAEYC. May 4, 2017. http://hello.naeyc.org/communities/all-discussions/printmessage ?MessageKey=e9df4ca7-d516-4e51-a465-b8e72a7b6de8.

Angelou, Maya. 2014. "Maya Angelou's last words: 'Listen to yourself and in that quietude you might hear the voice of God.'" *Catholic Online*. May 28. www .catholic.org/news/hf/faith/story.php?id=55580.

Beck, Martha. 2018. "3 Words That Will Help You Comfort Anyone." *Oprah.com*. Accessed February 13. www.oprah.com/inspiration/how-to-comfort-people.

Covey, Stephen R., A. Roger Merrill, and Rebecca R. Merrill. 1994. *First Things First: To Live, to Love, to Learn, to Leave a Legacy*. New York: Simon and Schuster.

Curtis, Deb. 2017. *Really Seeing Children: A Collection of Teaching and Learning Stories*. Lincoln, WA: Exchange Press.

Edelman, Marian Wright. 1992. *The Measure of Our Success: A Letter to My Children and Yours*. Boston: Beacon Press.

Greenleaf, Robert. www.greenleaf.org.

Haden, Jeff. 2013. "8 Ways to Be a Truly Memorable Boss." *Inc.com*. www.inc.com /jeff-haden/8-ways-to-be-memorable-boss.html.

hooks, bell. 1993. *Sisters of the Yam: Black Women and Self-Recovery*. Cambridge, MA: South End Press.

———. 2009. *Reel to Real: Race, Sex and Class at the Movies*. New York: Routledge.

National Head Start Association. 2018. *In Memoriam: Vanessa Rich, Lifelong Advocate*. Accessed February 14. www.nhsa.org/vanessa-rich-leadership-fund.

Obama, Barack. 2015. "Transcript: Obama Delivers Eulogy for Charleston Pastor, the Rev. Clementa Pinckney." June 26. *Washington Post*. www.washingtonpost. com/news/post-nation/wp/2015/06/26/transcript-obama-delivers-eulogy-for-charleston-pastor-the-rev-clementa-pinckney/?utm_term=.f7ad921b8ce6.

Pierre, Milca. 2016. "Meet the First Black Woman to Ever Run for President." *The Source*. February 3. http://thesource.com/2016/02/03/meet-the-first-black -woman-to-ever-run-for-president.

Rooke, David, and William R. Torbert. 2005. "Seven Transformations of Leadership." *Harvard Business Review*. April. https://hbr.org/2005/04/seven-transformations -of-leadership.

Schwartz, Tony. 2012. "What Women Know about Leadership that Men Don't." *Harvard Business Review*. October 30. https://hbr.org/2012/10/what-women -know-that-men-dont.

Sullivan, Debra Ren-Etta. 2009. "Lifting as You Climb. *Exchange Magazine*, March/April: 6–9.

Sykes, Maurice. 2014. *Doing the Right Thing for Children: Eight Qualities of Leadership*. St. Paul, MN: Redleaf Press.

Vanzant, Iyanla. 1998. *One Day My Soul Just Opened Up*. New York: Simon & Schuster.

Walker, Alice. 1983. *In Search of Our Mothers' Gardens: Womanist Prose*. New York: Houghton Mifflin Harcourt.

Winfrey, Oprah. 2011. "When People Show You Who They Are, Believe Them." *Oprah's Life Class,* October 26. www.oprah.com/oprahs-lifeclass/when-people -show-you-who-they-are-believe-them-video.